The
Real
Wood
Bible

The Real Wood Bible

The complete illustrated
guide to choosing and using
100 decorative woods

Nick Gibbs

FIREFLY BOOKS

A FIREFLY BOOK

Published by Firefly Books Ltd. 2005

Copyright © 2005 Quarto Inc.

Fifth printing, 2010

Published in the United States by
Firefly Books (U.S.) Inc.
P.O. Box 1338, Ellicott Station
Buffalo, New York 14205

Published in Canada by
Firefly Books Ltd.
66 Leek Crescent
Richmond Hill, Ontario L4B 1H1

Conceived, designed and produced by
Quarto Publishing plc
The Old Brewery
6 Blundell Street
London N7 9BH
United Kingdom

Publisher Cataloging-in-Publication Data (U.S.)

Gibbs, Nick
Real wood bible : the complete illustrated guide to choosing and using 100 decorative woods / Nick Gibbs. 1st ed.
[256] p. : col. ill. ; cm.
Includes index.
Summary: A resource for working with wood, and the various types of wood.
ISBN-13: 978-1-55407-033-6 (spiral)
ISBN-10: 1-55407-033-3 (spiral)
1. Wood. 2. Woodwork--Amateurs' manuals. I. Title.
674.8 22   TT180.G533 2005

Library and Archives Canada Cataloguing in Publication

Gibbs, Nick
Real wood bible : the complete illustrated guide to choosing and using 100 decorative woods / Nick Gibbs.
Includes index.
ISBN-13: 978-1-55407-033-6 (spiral)
ISBN-10: 1-55407-033-3 (spiral)
1. Woodwork. 2. Wood. I. Title.
TT180.G52 2005 684'.08   C2004-905963-7

QUAR.RWB

Project Editor: Paula McMahon
Art Editor: Claire Van Rynn
Senior Art Editor: Penny Cobb
Designer: Andrew Easton
Photographer: Paul Forrester
Picture Researcher: Claudia Tate
Copy Editor: Stuart Cooper

Art Director: Moira Clinch
Publisher: Piers Spence

Manufactured by Universal Graphic Pte Ltd, Singapore
Printed in China by Midas Printing International

684.08
GIB

2/24/11 BT 29.95

Contents

Wood Directory

Introduction

Most woodworkers have a "palette" of woods that they favor, experimenting with alternatives for a specific purpose, or perhaps because they come across or are given a new board or veneer. Cabinetmakers choose stable boards for panels, ideally quartersawn, that will not bend and buckle, or they glue decorative veneer to man-made sheets. Chairmakers select strong, long-grained woods for the legs and rails, but more decorative, softer lumber for the seat. Though carvers like ornate wood, and can carve almost anything with modern rotary tools, they prefer it to be even-grained to reduce the risk of tearing. Woodturners, though, will use almost anything, particularly if the grain and color are distinctive and will enhance the perfectly formed curves of their bowls and boxes.

Whether forced by the requirements of a particular project or just because of boredom with what is in the workshop, every woodworker comes to a point when it's time to try a new type of lumber. Today, thankfully, there is plenty to choose from. Veneers and turning blanks are easy to source and purchase by mail order, from a catalogue or over the Internet, and even boards can be ordered this way.

Each wood has its own distinctive characteristics, though of course many share similar colors, grain patterns or textures. Hardwoods are favored for their strength, decorative effects, wide range of colors and durability. Softwoods tend to be cheaper, and are often seen as functional materials for building and construction.

Distinctive grain, such as that shown in this ancient Bristlecone pine (below), is prized by woodturners, who will aim to preserve as much as possible of the character of the tree in their finished piece.

Wood is one of the most versatile of materials: in the hands of a skilled worker (right) it is transformed from a utilitarian building product into a thing of beauty.

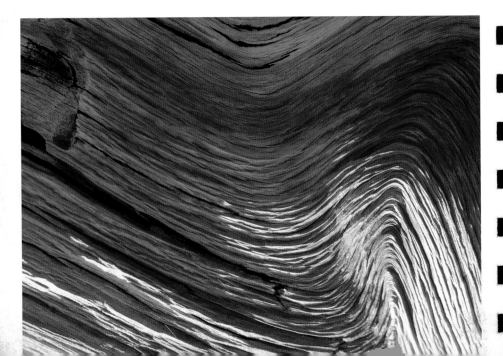

THE IDEAL LUMBER

Somewhere out there is the perfect lumber that is easy and pleasurable to work while also being visually interesting. The ideal lumber will also

1. have generally straight grain;
2. be close-grained and hard for a good finish, or coarse-grained and easy to bring to a high luster;
3. possess a few defects to add character without raising wastage rates to too high a level;
4. have a distinctive color and figure (pattern).

THE FAMILY OF WOODS

Look through the list of woods in this book and you will notice that some botanical and common names keep cropping up. There is an oak on almost every continent; indeed, that wood has been a giant of the lumber world for centuries. Other species that have dominated furniture making include the temperate hardwoods elm, ash and beech, and from the tropics, mahogany, teak and rosewood.

It is possible to argue that nearly all other woods are merely alternatives to these favored few, with lesser-known species gaining in popularity because of shortages or changing tastes. Woods of the genus *Acer* – maple and sycamore – are preferred for their close grain, ease of use and pale color, while cherry offers some of the qualities of mahogany but comes from a more trustworthy source. The huge number of tropical hardwoods now available perhaps reflects the attempt to find weather-resistant species to replace endangered woods such as teak, or furniture-quality species to replicate mahogany. Often they are poor imitations – in terms of color, figure and ease of use – of the originals, and that perhaps explains why temperate hardwoods like cherry have become so popular. Of course, tropical hardwoods are still favored in many cases for windows, doors and other joinery.

The most exotic species, such as rosewood and ebony, are now very expensive, and tend to be used only for decorative effects or as veneer. A by-product of the environmental movement has been the introduction of small quantities of previously unheard-of woods, many of them harvested by communal forestry enterprises in the tropics. Some of these are exquisite in color and figure, but as yet hardly used.

Plantations of conifers (below left) provide the world's chipboard and constructional softwood. Temperate hardwoods are sourced from northern hemisphere forests, which often contain a mix of broadleaf species (below right). Manufacturers are increasingly turning to tropical hardwoods for contemporary furniture (right).

HOW TO CHOOSE WOOD

There are many factors to consider when choosing wood. If there is a strict budget to watch then price is a significant issue, and the degree of wastage may also be important. The structure of the piece may limit the range of options, depending on whether the design needs hardness, strength or a bit of give. A solid tabletop is best made from woods that are not likely to move, as are drawer components, which need to fit well for years.

Color may be important, either to match existing furniture, or to enhance the specific design. Stains and dyes can help, though many woodworkers prefer the integrity of an unadulterated finish. You may need to consider grain pattern and figure. Though it is often tempting to use the most decorative woods you can find, sometimes intricate designs demand less sophisticated surface effects. In contrast, a simple design can be raised to new heights by a unique piece of lumber.

Texture can be used as creatively as color and figure. Coarse-grained species like oak and elm can be sandblasted or wire-brushed, and then limed or stained for dramatic effects, while highly polished rosewood is spectacular for more formal work. Species with contrasting colors, textures and patterns can be juxtaposed successfully, but usually need some form of visual buffer between them, and great care needs to be taken when attempting to form unlikely partnerships.

When choosing your wood, keep the task in mind. A decorative piece would benefit from a wood of beautiful color and texture, which may be expensive.

For garden furniture your requirements are different – you need a strong, durable wood that takes preservatives well.

SEVEN STEPS TO CHOOSING WOOD FOR A PROJECT

1. Establish how much lumber you need, based on the design.
2. Consider the eventual setting for the item in terms of style, color and texture. A plain, Shaker-style interior is likely to demand less conspicuous species such as maples, cherries, fruitwoods and birches. Most exotic hardwoods, especially from tropical forests, will suit a more formal, ornamental setting, while coarse-grained oak, elm and ash have a softer visual effect that works well in a less formal space.
3. When necessary, choose woods by function: ash for bending, ebony for edge features or bandings, aromatic cedar for drawer bottoms (it will retain a fresh smell and deter bugs). You can fight a wood's natural inclinations, like trying to bend balsa, but invariably the results will be unsuccessful and the effort frustrating. Some woods do not take to glue so well, while others need special finishing treatments.
4. Some species are available only in limited dimensions. You will not find many long, straight pieces of boxwood, though it is excellent for tool handles, nor wide boards of ebony, which turners adore. If a wood is not available in thicknesses greater than 1 inch it will not be easy to use for a tabletop. Of course, modern adhesives enable us to build up sections of almost any wood, as long as the grain is not so distinctive that the joins are obvious.
5. Talk to fellow woodworkers and consult this book to find suitable species. Check if lumber is available from a certified sustainable source.
6. Though woodworkers should always take the necessary safety precautions, find out the potential risks of using a particular wood. The dust of many woods can aggravate breathing and cause skin allergies or problems.
7. Having narrowed down your options, start hunting high and low for what you want, beginning with your local supplier. If all else fails, check the alternatives listed for most species in the Wood Directory that forms the main part of this book.

WORKING SAFELY

When working with wood, always take precautions against accidents with machinery. Use ear protection and eye shields, and a mask or respirator to keep dust from your nose and lungs (left). Some species are hated for the noxious power of their dust, which causes respiratory and skin problems or exacerbates existing allergies.

Make sure to investigate the health hazards before using a particular wood. Specific species have not been noted as harmful because reports are anecdotal, and evidence linked to particular woods hasn't been found. It would be irresponsible to list harmful woods as some harmful species may inadvertently be missed. Woodworkers should be cautious and make a note of any effects they may suffer from wood they are using. See a doctor if symptoms appear.

Eye, nose and mouth protection is always sensible (as well as protecting ears from high noise), but you should also limit the amount of dust you produce to a minimum. This can be done by avoiding sanding operations as much as possible, and by connecting all machines and power tools to extraction systems. You can also acquire ambient dust filters that remove the finest particles.

Sustainability

Wood is an extraordinary material, probably the most versatile of all. It is strong, available in many sizes, flexible, beautiful and relatively easy to use. Above all, though, it is renewable, at least in principle. The trouble is that for decades, if not centuries, people have cut down the forests and squandered the returns without a care for the consequences.

Concern about the destruction of forests began to grow in the 1980s, when various nongovernmental organizations such as Green Cross, Rainforest Alliance, Friends of the Earth, Greenpeace and the World Wildlife Fund (WWF) highlighted the plight of tropical forests. These bodies have drawn attention both to the extinction of species and to the gradual transformation of forest into desert. Significant research has been done by the World Conservation Monitoring Centre (WCMC) and the International Union for Conservation of Nature and Natural Resources (IUCN). The International Tropical Timber Organization (ITTO) is a further valuable resource for anyone concerned about the status of the lumber they buy. Finally, the Convention on International Trade in Endangered Species (CITES) tracks endangered woods that are sold commercially.

Though logging, legal or otherwise, has always been an issue, it is the attempted conversion of forests into farmland that is largely to blame for their destruction. The

*Logs from an FSC-certified source are stamped with the organization's symbol (**left**). This guarantees that the lumber has been produced in a sustainable manner, most likely from a managed forest (**above**), where a program of planting ensure that trees are replaced with saplings as they are harvested.*

ecosystem in tropical rain forests relies on trees to protect the fragile soil and provide nutrients from decaying wood and leaves. Once the trees are gone, the soil cannot support agriculture for very long and the consequence is spreading desertification.

As a result of campaigns by environmental groups, demand has grown for lumber from sustainable sources.

The Forest Stewardship Council (FSC) and other organizations support enterprises aiming to manage their forests with a long-term view. To promote good forest management worldwide, FSC has ensured that its principles also apply to temperate forests of all sorts, with producers in North America and Scandinavia selling a growing quantity of certified lumber from private, public and communal forests. Ironically, FSC certification has proved far easier to achieve for temperate forests than for tropical rain forests, and so has given a competitive advantage to the very hemisphere that needs it least.

HOW DOES CERTIFICATION WORK?

The FSC's program is the most prominent certification program for lumber, though other organizations have their own schemes. The bulk of environmental groups, including Rainforest Alliance and Forest Ethics, promote the FSC program and logo, and point consumers toward certified suppliers.

Third-party certifiers, such as Smartwood, SGS and other organizations around the world, follow FSC guidelines in auditing forest enterprises, lumber processors and manufacturers of wood-based products. Once certified, a company can use the FSC logo on specific products or across its entire range, depending on the results of the audit. Other certification schemes may be less well known, but still represent valuable steps in the right direction. They include, in abbreviated form, CSA, MTCC, SFI, PEFC and LEI (see glossary for full names).

ENDANGERED TREE SPECIES

Most concerned woodworkers see it as their responsibility to determine the status of the lumber they use, and buying FSC-certified wood is considered a reliable approach. But the range of available species is still limited, with certification very difficult in some parts of the world.

Clearing the forests of trees is bad enough, but the ultimate consequences of out-of-control logging are far

SPECIES TO WATCH OUT FOR

Species appearing in the CITES Appendices do change from time to time, but the following have featured consistently and are pinpointed by various organizations as suspect. Find a certified source for these lumbers, or use an alternative species.

Brazilian rosewood (*Dalbergia nigra*)	AI
Lignum vitae (*Guaiacum officinale*)	AII, EN
Mahogany (*Swietenia* species)	AII
Afrormosia (*Pericopsis elata*)	AII, EN
Keruing (*Dipterocarpus* species)	CR, EN
Cedar (West Indian) (*Cedrela odorata*)	EN, VU, AIII
Ebony (*Diospyros* species)	EN, VU
Makore (*Tieghemella* species)	EN
Wenge (*Millettia laurentii*)	EN
Meranti (*Shorea* species)	CR and EN
Agba (*Gossweilerodendron balsamiferum*)	EN

Key		
AI	=	CITES Appendix I
AII	=	CITES Appendix II
AIII	=	CITES Appendix III
CR	=	IUCN Red List, Critically Endangered
EN	=	IUCN Red List, Endangered
VU	=	IUCN Red List, Vulnerable

worse, and have brought some species close to extinction. A number of organizations keep track of species considered at risk of extinction. Foremost among these is CITES, which produces three lists, or Appendices, of endangered woods sold commercially.

Species listed in CITES Appendix I are defined as "threatened by extinction." It also notes that they "are or may be threatened by trade." Brazilian rosewood (*Dalbergia nigra*) is one of the better-known species listed in CITES Appendix I. It should be avoided (and is in any case unobtainable except from old or recycled stock).

Species in Appendix II are endangered and their trade is controlled, with exporters having to certify that the lumber has been legally logged and sustainably harvested. Since suppliers' claims of sustainability are not always entirely trustworthy, however, we would recommend buying only those woods with FSC certification, which is more stringent than CITES. You might also study the IUCN Red List to research which species are considered to be at risk. The Global Trees campaign profiles species that are threatened, explaining why they are in danger and how they might be saved.

Temperate species are not threatened by extinction in the same way, though campaigns have been fought against the felling of ancient or old-growth forests. For many woodworkers, however, the easy option is to buy temperate zone lumber, certified or not, and avoid tropical species altogether. Yet forests depend on earnings for survival, and buying exotic wood from reliable sources encourages sustainable harvesting, and protects the rain forests from conversion into something more immediately profitable.

RECYCLE OLD WOOD

Recycling discarded lumber from old furniture and buildings is both sensible and economical. The wood will be seasoned and conditioned to its environment, unless it has been left to rot outside. This is about the only way

A reclaimed wooden floor (left) is fashionable, hardwearing, full of character, and good for the environment! This rustic chest (right) is not pretty, but its 100-year-old pine is sound, and ripe for remodeling into something more contemporary.

you will find some of the rarest woods, such as Cuban mahogany and Brazilian rosewood. Cabinets, tables and chests that no longer suit contemporary tastes can be converted into beautiful modern furniture.

Many salvage yards sell recycled materials. Forest Ethics lists some of them by region across the United States. By using reclaimed wood you can be sure that no trees have been illegally or unnecessarily felled.

WOODWORKING WITH A CONSCIENCE

Here are the steps to take when considering what to buy with sustainability in mind:

1. If you plan to use a tropical hardwood, check its endangered status in the Wood Directory in this book, or consult the lists produced by environmental groups. If it is at risk, buy only FSC-certified lumber, or choose an alternative that is not endangered.
2. Though temperate forests generally do not face the same threats as forests in the tropics, always consider buying temperate hardwoods and softwoods that are certified. This is good for your peace of mind, helps to raise awareness and is useful as a marketing device.
3. Ask your supplier questions about the status of the lumber you are considering buying. This helps to raise awareness and encourages merchants to check the sources of their products.
4. Consider using recycled materials of your own or bought from salvage yards in the form of boards or furniture that can be dismantled.

KNOWLEDGE BANK

The following web sites give more information on sustainability and endangered species

CITES Appendices I and II
www.cites.org
ForestEthics
www.forestethics.org
Forest Stewardship Council
www.fscus.org
FSC International
www.fsc.org
Global Trees Campaign
www.globaltrees.org
Good Wood Guide
www.foe.co.uk/pubsinfo/pubscat/practical.html
International Tropical Timber Organization
www.itto.or.jp
IUCN Red List of Threatened Species
www.redlist.org
Rainforest Alliance
www.rainforest-alliance.org

Buying Wood

However much the Internet has changed the way we buy woodworking tools, the lumberyard or home center remains the most popular place to purchase wood. The chain stores and contractors' yards supply both home improvement enthusiasts and the building trade, and stock mainly surfaced and rough-sawn softwoods, with a limited range of planed hardwood boards.

For a wider selection of hardwoods you might need to travel to a specialist woodworkers' yard or a dealer in fine hardwoods. Finding a supplier of local or imported temperate hardwoods should not prove too difficult, as 20 or so species are commonly available. There are far fewer retailers of high-value exotics. For small quantities or for veneers, buying over the Internet or from a catalogue may prove cost-effective, but start by ordering only small quantities to test the service and quality.

PLANED OR SAWN?

Boards are supplied either ready-planed or straight from the saw, the latter being used largely by the construction industry. Softwoods, in particular, are available in standard dimensions, referred to as either nominal or dressed (see page 18). The nominal dimension relates to the sawn sizes of a board and the dressed dimension refers to the size of the board after it has been surface planed. When you buy planed lumber the yard will usually refer to the nominal size, but not always. Some mail order businesses now state the dressed sizes.

Hardwoods sold in home centers will be Surfaced Four Sides (S4S). You can also buy hardwoods Surfaced Two Sides (S2S), with the other edges left unplaned. When you buy from a local sawmill or a specialist hardwood supplier the boards will often be rough-sawn, with no planed faces or edges, so it is more difficult to judge the quality, color and figure. The thicknesses and widths will also vary depending on how the tree was processed.

The fastest way to surface rough-sawn wood is with a jointer or thickness planer. If you don't own one, then buying ready planed lumber may be your only option,

DRESSED HARDWOOD

Standard thicknesses of dressed hardwood in inches

Nominal	Dressed
1	c. 3/4
1½	c. 1¼–1⅜
2	1¾–1⅞
2½	2¼–2⅜
3	2¾–2⅞
4	3¾–3⅞

Hardwood logs marked for quality and stacked ready for sawing into boards.

unless you particularly enjoy surface planing by hand! But planed wood is more expensive than sawn lumber, as you are paying for the labor of machining it and the sawdust that goes to waste. You may be more efficient at preparing boards in your own workshop, wasting less wood and achieving exactly the dimensions you need. Ready-planed lumber may continue to move as it adjusts to your workshop, and may need more machining after it has become conditioned.

STRAIGHT-EDGED OR WANEY?

All softwoods and most hardwoods are supplied straight-edged, making it very simple to estimate how much you need. Some local hardwoods sold straight from the mill, and even some imported hardwoods from Europe, may have one or two waney (irregular) edges, often with the bark still attached. For waney-edged boards the yard will normally measure the widest and narrowest points and average out the width, but watch out for boards with unusable defects and wide bands of sapwood so you do not pay for waste wood.

PAYING FOR LUMBER

Softwood comes in a defined range of standard widths and thicknesses, so its price is usually determined by length, in 1-foot or 1-inch intervals. This is known as a linear price – it is said to be sold by the linear foot – and suits boards of standard machined sizes.

The size of hardwood boards varies widely depending on the species and the source, so they are normally priced by volume as a board foot (that is, 12 inches x 12 inches x 1 inch), which is one-twelfth of a cubic foot, or 144 cubic inches. To calculate the cost of a board, multiply the thickness by the width and then the length, and then divide by 144.

For longer pieces, when it is easier to think in feet than inches, use feet for the length but inches for the thickness and width, and then divide by 12 instead of 144.

The logs have been sawn to boards but left with a waney edge.

Boards surfaced on all sides (S4S) and stacked ready for sale.

NOMINAL AND DRESSED SIZES

Buying wood can be complicated by the terminology used for dimensions. For rough-sawn hardwoods and softwoods it is a case of what you see is what you get, with a 6 x 1-inch board measuring exactly that. The dimensions of planed boards often refer to the nominal size, which is the width and thickness of the board before it was planed. The dressed size may actually be anything up to 1/4 inch less than that.

When buying planed softwood boards you may ask for the nominal size but receive the dressed size. The difference is either 1/4 inch, 1/2 inch or 3/4 inch. Most softwoods are sold in nominal 1-inch and 2-inch thicknesses, and in widths ranging from 2 inches to 12 inches.

WASTAGE

Always buy more lumber than you need for a project because there will certainly be wastage and you may make mistakes. Remember that you will lose up to 1/4 inch off the thickness when planing sawn boards in the workshop. Sapwood and defects may also increase

DRESSED SOFTWOODS

Common dimensions of softwoods (inches)

Nominal	Dressed
1 x 1	3/4 x 3/4
1 x 2	3/4 x 1 1/2
1 x 3	3/4 x 2 1/2
1 x 4	3/4 x 3 1/2
1 x 6	3/4 x 5 1/2
1 x 8	3/4 x 7 1/4
1 x 10	3/4 x 9 1/4
1 x 12	3/4 x 11 1/4
2 x 1	1 1/2 x 3/4
2 x 2	1 1/2 x 1 1/2
2 x 3	1 1/2 x 2 1/2
2 x 4	1 1/2 x 3 1/2
2 x 6	1 1/2 x 5 1/2
2 x 8	1 1/2 x 7 1/4
2 x 10	1 1/2 x 9 1/4
2 x 12	1 1/2 x 11 1/4

the wastage rates, which can vary from 20 to 40 percent, depending on the species and grade and whether you buy S4S or rough-sawn boards.

Gluing up wide panels from a series of strips is costly in terms of time and sawdust, but will produce more stable panels. It can also be efficient if it enables you to use odd bits that would otherwise be too thin or too narrow.

LUMBER GRADING

Hardwood lumber is graded by the size and number of clean cuts that can be taken from a board, in order to estimate the yield, to standards set by the U.S. National Hardwood Lumber Association. The best-quality hardwood lumber is referred to as firsts and seconds, which are technically separate categories, but usually combined as FAS. An FAS board must be at least 6 inches wide and 8 feet long, yielding at least 83 1/3 percent clear face, making such lumber ideal for cabinetry and fine furniture making.

Where a wood is difficult to obtain in wide boards, good results can be obtained by gluing up a number of smaller widths. The resulting board is stable and resists warping.

Use this checklist to ensure that you leave the yard with what you need and not a carload of useless boards, or even worse, not quite enough.

1. Make a cutting list of every piece of lumber needed for your project and convert this into a bill of materials, based on your knowledge of the lengths, widths and thicknesses of boards you can source. Length is the critical dimension: boards can be glued up to be wider and thicker but rarely longer.
2. Ensure that the bill of materials includes a wastage and mistakes factor of about 30 percent so that you have plenty of extra lumber.
3. When buying planed boards make sure you find out whether your supplier is specifying the nominal size or the dressed size so you can be sure of what you are buying.
4. Check boards carefully for defects, particularly knots and checks, that might affect what you can use. Once again, length is usually the most important dimension.
5. Look out for distorted boards. You can normally work with cupped wood by cutting it along its length and re-gluing to make panels. Bowed wood is fine if you will be cutting the board into shorter lengths. Twist, though, should be avoided unless the board is to be crosscut to much shorter lengths.
6. Take care when handling the wood: a dent at a critical point can affect how you process the boards. Be careful where you insert the points of a moisture meter, finding somewhere you know will not be important in the finished work, ideally in freshly cut end-grain.

In a similar way the next two grades, Selects and No.1 Common, are sometimes grouped as No.1 Common and Better. These are seen as a good alternative to FAS if only one clean face is needed, or when smaller pieces are likely to be cut.

Most softwood for woodworkers is known as construction lumber, particularly the "yard lumber" grades, which are graded for appearance rather than strength. These include the Nos.1–5 Common grades and the Finish Appearance and Select Appearance lumber grades, which are all judged by the number and size of defects and knots on their better side, rather than on the poorer side, as is the case for hardwoods. Most woodworkers tend to use Appearance lumber for projects and Common lumber for DIY tasks like shelving, paneling and interior joinery. The best grades of Appearance lumber are known as Finish and Selects, and stock that has been pre-molded or surfaced on all four sides (S4S) falls within this category.

Stacks of S4S lumber, graded and marked for quality, in a lumberyard.

ABBREVIATIONS USED IN THE LUMBER INDUSTRY

This list includes most common abbreviations; more can be found on Web site: www.woodbin.com

BUYING

ADF	after deducting freight
AL	all lengths
AV	average
AW	all widths
AW&L	all widths and lengths
BD	board
BD FT	board foot/feet
BDL	bundle
BL	bill of lading
CC	cubical content
cft, cu.ft.	cubic foot or feet
CIFE	cost, insurance, freight and exchange
C/L	carload
DIM	dimension
E	edge
ED	equivalent defects
FA	facial area
FBM, Ft.BM	feet board measure
FOB	free on board
FRT	freight
FT, ft.	foot or feet
FT. SM	feet surface measure
G	girth
GM	grade marked
Hdwd.	hardwood
H&M	hit and miss
H or M	hit or miss
IN, in.	inch or inches
LBR, Lbr	lumber
LCL	less than carload
LGR	longer
LGTH	length
Lft, Lf, 1in. ft	lineal foot or feet
LIN, Lin	lineal

M	thousand
MBM, MBF,	thousand (feet)
M.BM	board measure
Mft	thousand feet
MW	mixed widths
NBM	net board measure
No.	number
Ord	order
Pcs.	pieces
R/L, RL	random lengths
R/W, RW	random widths
Sftwd.	softwood
SM	surface measure
Specs	specifications
Std. lgths	standard lengths
STK	stock
TBR	timber
WDR, wdr	wider
WT	weight
WTH	width

GRADING

AD	air-dried
B1S	bead one side
B2S	bead two sides
B&B, B&BTR	B and better
BEV	bevel or beveled
BH	boxed heart
BSND	bright sapwood no defect
BTR	better
CB	center-beaded
CG2E	center groove on two edges
CLR	clear
CM	center-matched
CV	center V
DKG	decking
D1S	dressed one side, see S1S, etc.
FAS	firsts and seconds

FAS1F	firsts and seconds one face	STR, STRUCT	structural
FG	flat or slash grain	S&E	surfaced side and edge
FLG	flooring	S1E	surfaced one edge
FOHC	free of heart center	S2E	surfaced two edges
FOK	free of knots	S1S	surfaced one side
FURN	furniture stock	S2S	surfaced two sides
G or GR	green	S4S	surfaced four sides
Hrt	heart	S1S&CM	surfaced one side and center matched
J&P	joists and planks	S1S1E	surfaced one side and one edge
JTD	jointed	S2S&SL	surfaced two sides and shiplapped
KD	kiln-dried	T&G	tongued and grooved
MC, M.C.	moisture content	UTIL	utility
MCO	mill culls out	VG	vertical (edge) grain
MG	medium grain or mixed grain	WHAD	worm holes a defect
MLDG, Mldg	molding	WHND	worm holes no defect
M-S	mixed species		
MSR	machine stress-rated		
N	nosed	**SPECIES**	
P	planed	AF	alpine fir
PAD	partially air-dried	DF	Douglas fir
PE	plain end	DF-L	Douglas fir, larch
PET	precision end trimmed	ES	Engelmann spruce
Qtd.	quartered	HEM	hemlock
RDM	random	IC	incense cedar
REG, Reg	regular	IWP	Idaho white pine
RES	resawn	L	western larch
RGH, Rgh	rough	LP	lodgepole pine
S-DRY	surfaced dry (19% MC or less)	MH	mountain hemlock
SE	square edge	PP	ponderosa pine
SEL, Sel	select or select grade	SIT. SPR, SS	Sitka spruce
SE&S	square edge and sound	SP	sugar pine
SG	slash or flat grain	SYP	southern pine
S-GRN	surfaced green (more than 19% MC)	WC	western cedar
SGSSND	sapwood, gum spots and streaks, no defects	WCH	West Coast hemlock
		WCW	West Coast woods
SQ	square	WF	white fir
SQRS	squares	WRC	western red cedar
SR	stress-rated	WW	white woods
SSND	sap stain no defect	YP	yellow pine
STD. M	standard matched		
STD, Std	standard		

Trees to Boards

To understand the dynamics of a board it helps to understand how a tree grows. Roots act as an anchor to hold the tree upright, and they also absorb mineral-rich moisture. The sap is drawn up through the outer layer of the wood, or cambium, which is just below the bark, to the thirsty leaves, where moisture evaporates. The leaves absorb carbon dioxide, and with the help of sunlight, convert it into nutrients for growth through photosynthesis.

The cells in the cambium are designed to carry or store sap in their early years, and are transformed with time into the strong backbone of the tree. During spring and early summer, when the tree is growing, the cells are relatively large and full of sap to feed the tree. They work as a series of tiny interlocking tubes, with the sap winding its way upward from one cell to the next. Later in the year the cells are thinner with denser walls, being used only to carry moisture and strengthen the tree. Though the sap and nutrients move largely up the tree, there is some dissipation toward the center through cells known as medullary rays, which lie at right angles to the rings and can produce colorful figuring when exposed on quartersawn boards.

Sectioned trunk (below) showing growth rings, medullary rays and the darker heartwood at the center. This board (right) *has been sliced vertically: the heartwood lies toward the bottom, the sapwood in a band at the top edge.*

Just as a new layer of early and late sapwood grows each year, so another layer, nearer the center, is transformed into heartwood to support the tree. We can thank that transformation for the remarkable strength of lumber, and the annual buildup of growth rings provides us with a method for aging a tree or even a board. The proportion of sapwood and heartwood in a tree remains constant throughout its life, while right at the center the cells decay and often suffer from fungal attack. And though it might ultimately kill the tree, that decay can cause all sorts of special effects in lumber, with oak turning darker brown and the heart of ash often acquiring olive streaks.

CHARACTERISTICS OF LUMBER

No two types of lumber are the same, each being distinguished by a complex mix of characteristics. These distinctions can be determined by the genetics of a species, and be common to all examples of that type of tree, or by the circumstances of growth, soil type or climate, and therefore particular and exclusive to one individual specimen.

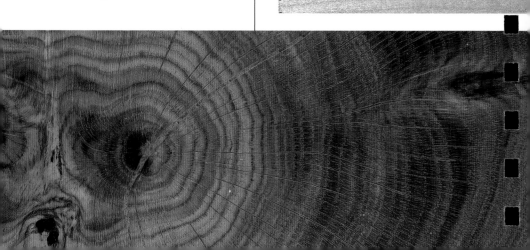

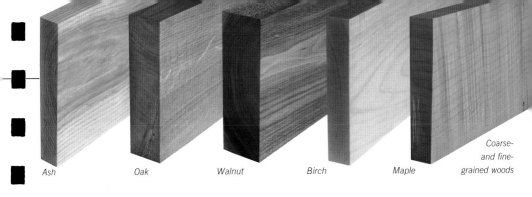

Ash   Oak   Walnut   Birch   Maple   *Coarse- and fine-grained woods*

HEARTWOOD AND SAPWOOD

The proportion of sapwood to heartwood varies from species to species. Prized for its purple-brown color, exquisite sweeping grain and even texture, English walnut (*Juglans regia*) has a frustratingly wide, soft band of pale sapwood that is good for almost nothing. The contrast between the sap and the heart of English yew (*Taxus baccata*) is just as distinct, but is used by many woodworkers as a feature.

Other woods, particularly the tropical species, have little discernible sapwood, and for some the transition between heartwood and sapwood is so gradual and indistinct that much of the sapwood can be safely used for woodwork. But find out first. The heart of oak, for instance, is fairly resistant to insect attack, but the sapwood is too tasty to resist and is often riddled with holes.

GRAIN

Woodworkers never stop talking about the grain of a wood. They endlessly debate its varying qualities and challenges, forever comparing the benefits of one against the pitfalls of another. There are, however, three major issues to consider when studying the grain of a wood: the texture, the consistency and the direction.

Grain texture

Most woods are described as being either coarse (or open) grained or fine (or close) grained, though many are somewhere in between. Coarse-grained woods, such as oak, ash or walnut, have fewer, larger cells to carry the sap, and this results in large, open pores on the surface of the wood that have to be filled with some kind of compound to obtain a perfectly flat finish. Plenty of woodworkers prefer such woods, and highlight their characteristics by sandblasting the surface or wire-brushing. Close-grained woods, such as birch or maple, have thinner cells, and many more of them. This makes them easier to bring to a high, blemish-free finish, though a soft close-grained wood will not have much luster (the quality of wood that makes the surface shine). Yew, despite having a close, even texture and consistent grain, is very difficult to use because its grain is interlocking and shoots off in all directions.

Grain consistency

The lines of grain you see on a board are created by the contrast between the large, thin-walled cells that are formed in the early growing season of the year and the denser, darker latewood that comprises narrower cells with thicker walls. In tropical forests, where temperatures are even throughout the year, the contrast between earlywood and latewood is only slight, and such lumbers are often favored for their even grain and for their consistency. That does not mean they are always easy to use, however, as the texture may be coarse or the grain interlocked, or both. In temperate regions the contrast between earlywood and later growth is more significant, being both pleasing to the eye and occasionally frustrating to work. The contrast in density can make the lumber difficult to cut and plane, with tools jumping as they hit a harder layer, and saws and chisels diverted wildly from their true course.

Grain direction

The direction of the grain differs from species to species, and sometimes from one tree to the next. The finest woods, such as white oak (*Quercus alba*) and black walnut (*Juglans nigra*), are favored for their straight grain, created by cells growing in line with one another, all pointing upward to the sky. Even those species genetically disposed to straightness can be sent off in all directions by poor woodland management, and while forests comprising a jumble of flora and fauna are valued for their biodiversity, they do not always produce valuable straight-grained trees. Even when the grain is straight, this does not mean it is consistent or evenly textured, but any good sawmill should be able to keep the grain parallel to the length of a board. The woodworker's saw or plane can then cut or slice along the grain without suddenly tearing the wood as the grain alters direction.

Other woods, like chestnut, tend to have spiraling grain, which can be observed from the outside of the tree. This is much more difficult to manage, so it devalues the lumber. The most challenging lumbers, from the woodworker's perspective, have what is known as interlocking grain, with its direction almost impossible to predict. Just when you think you are planing happily with the grain, like brushing a horse, the direction suddenly changes and you find yourself working against the nap.

WHAT IS FIGURE?

Woodworkers sometimes talk about figure, describing one board as beautifully figured and the next as rather bland. The term relates to the combination of grain direction, texture and consistency that defines the look, feel and ease of use of a board. The figure can be determined by the way a board has been cut or milled, or by the twists and turns of growth within a tree.

HOW WOOD DRIES

Many people believe, because it continues to move, that lumber still lives after it has been converted into boards. In fact, any warping or bowing that occurs is a result of changes in moisture content as the wood dries or absorbs water vapor from the local environment. Once a tree is felled it is the responsibility of the forester, sawmill and woodworker to deal with the moisture content, gradually drying or seasoning the lumber to produce boards free of checks (cracks), cupping or twist.

As a felled tree trunk loses moisture it contracts, with cracks spreading out radially from the pith (the center of the log) if it is left too long. By cutting the roundwood (logs) into planks the sawmill releases the tension and allows the wood to contract more easily. The seasoning process requires great care: the wood must be stacked in a dry but well-ventilated site, with the boards separated by stickers (battens) to allow air to circulate between them. The drying process may be speeded up by using a kiln, of which there are various types. Painting or waxing the ends of boards ensures consistent conditioning along the length of a plank, though some cracking at the ends is to be expected, as the wood there dries faster than elsewhere.

SHRINKAGE RATES

Fortunately, wood moves hardly at all along its length as it dries. A board shrinks across its width and thickness, but not at the same rate. One of the reasons you see cracks in the end of a log is that the cells contract more around the rings (tangential movement) than from the center outward (radial movement). This has a significant impact on the way boards need to be planked (see Converting Trees into Boards, page 26).

The moisture content of wood is measured with a moisture meter, which displays the reading as a percentage. Air drying is likely to bring the moisture level in a board down to about 15 percent, depending on the species and conditions, with planks traditionally needing a year per inch of thickness to season. Wood for interior furniture and joinery in centrally heated houses and offices needs to be dried to about 10 percent moisture content, otherwise the maker cannot guarantee the joints

SHRINKAGE RATES OF COMMON WOODS

Shrinkage rates (%) of some common woods, from green to oven-dry (0%)
Source: United States Forest Products Laboratory (USFPL)

Lumber	Radial	Tangential	Lumber	Radial	Tangential
Afrormosia	3.0	6.4	Keruing	5.2	10.9
Alder, red	4.4	6.3	Larch, western	4.5	9.1
Ash, white	4.9	7.8	Lauan	4.4	5.4
Balsa	3.0	7.6	Mahogany, African	2.5	4.5
Basswood	6.6	9.3	Mahogany, American (true)	3.0	4.1
Beech	5.5	11.9	Oak, red (northern or southern)	4.0	8.6
Birch, paper	6.3	8.6	Oak, white	5.6	10.5
Birch, yellow	7.3	9.5	Obeche	3.1	5.3
Bubinga	5.8	8.4	Persimmon	7.9	11.2
Butternut	3.4	6.4	Pine, parana	4.0	7.9
Cedar, incense	3.3	5.2	Pine, pitch	4.0	7.1
Cedar, Port Orford	4.6	6.9	Pine, ponderosa	3.9	6.2
Cedar, West Indian	4.1	6.3	Pine, sugar	2.9	5.6
Cedar, western red	2.4	5.0	Pine, western white	4.1	7.4
Cherry, black (American)	3.7	7.1	Primavera	3.1	5.2
Chestnut, horse	2.0	3.0	Purpleheart	3.2	6.1
Chestnut (American)	3.4	6.7	Ramin	3.9	8.7
Cocobolo	3.0	4.0	Rosewood, Brazilian	2.9	4.6
Ebony	5.5	6.5	Rosewood, Indian	2.7	5.8
Elm	4.2	7.2	Sapele	4.6	8.0
Elm, cedar	4.7	10.2	Sassafras	4.0	6.2
Elm, rock	4.8	8.9	Satinwood, Ceylon	6.0	7.0
Fir, Douglas	4.8	7.5	Spruce, Sitka	4.3	7.5
Greenheart	8.2	9.0	Sycamore	5.0	8.4
Hemlock, western	4.2	7.8	Tanoak	4.9	11.7
Hickory	7.0	10.5	Teak	2.2	4.0
Holly	4.8	9.9	Virola	5.3	9.6
Iroko	2.8	3.8	Walnut, black	5.5	7.8
Jarrah	4.6	6.6	Walnut, English	4.3	6.4
Jelutong	2.0	4.0	Walnut, Queensland	5.0	9.0
Karri	7.2	10.7			

SHRINKAGE BY MOISTURE CONTENT

Shrinkage rates in inches across a 1-foot-wide board
Source: United States Forest Products Laboratory (USFPL)

Moisture content (%)	Radial shrinkage (inches)	Tangential shrinkage (inches)
25	0.1	0.15
20	0.2	0.30
15	0.35	0.50
10	0.42	0.70
5	0.60	0.85

will not loosen and the panels split once it is in the home. This final conditioning is usually achieved in workshop wood storage, under the woodworker's bed (where it is usually warm and dry) or in special kilns.

Different species of wood shrink by varying amounts as they dry. The chart (above) shows the average rates of shrinkage by moisture content across a board originally 1 foot wide.

SHRINKAGE IN THE WORKSHOP

For many woodworkers the critical measure is the shrinkage that occurs between the 20 percent moisture content of boards when they arrive in the workshop after air drying, and the 10 percent moisture content they need to have reached after assembly into furniture for use in a centrally heated home. The chart (right) shows radial and tangential shrinkage rates between these two moisture levels.

CONVERTING TREES INTO BOARDS

The challenge for the sawmill lies in maximizing the amount of saleable boards they can cut from a tree, aiming to find a balance between quality and quantity. The simplest technique is to slice the trunk into layers, anything between 1 inch and 4 inches thick, a method

known as through-and-through- or crown-cutting. Boards cut this way can be identified by curved rings at the ends that lie flat, and by the flame-shaped grain along the face of the board.

While crown-cutting may be economical, crown-cut boards often end up cupping (see page 28).

Because tangential movement is normally at least two-thirds greater than radial movement, woodworkers often favor boards with the rings at right angles to the face of the board. This way the most significant movement is across the thickness rather than the width, and there is less risk of cupping across the boards. Such boards are

SHRINKAGE IN THE WORKSHOP

Species	Radial shrinkage (%)	Tangential shrinkage (%)
Ash	1.3	1.8
Beech	1.7	3.2
Blackbean	1.0	2.0
Elm, English	1.5	2.4
Mahogany, American	1.0	1.3
Padauk	0.5	0.66
Teak	0.7	1.2
Oak, English	1.5	2.5
Oak, Japanese	1.0	2.8
Oak, Tasmanian	1.4	2.1
Maple, rock	1.8	2.6
Walnut, English	1.6	2.0

LUMBER MOISTURE CONTENT

Average values for specific purposes (%)

Pieces near direct heat	9
Furniture and interior fittings in highly heated areas	11
Projects for normally heated areas	12
Projects for occasionally heated areas such as bedrooms	13
Boat building	15
Garden furniture	16
Framework	22

referred to as quartersawn because the tree is often milled in quarters to achieve this result, which takes considerable time and skill and will often waste wood. Quartersawn lumber is given a high value both for its stability and, in some cases, for the distinctive medullary rays that are exposed by the technique.

COMMON PROBLEMS WITH BOARDS

Wood moves and can deteriorate during seasoning, and afterward in the workshop, as it adjusts to local conditions. Watch out for problems when buying lumber; some can be resolved but others make the boards very difficult to manage.

The sawyer must "read" the log as he cuts, making decisions on the basis of economy or appearance. Sometimes the two are the same thing: wide, knot-free boards (above). Or the sawyer may have to turn the log after the first cut to avoid the heart shake.

Methods of log conversion:
1 True radial cut
2 Plain-sawn
3 Quartersawn
4 Through-and-through or crown-cut
5 Billet-sawn
6 Cut for board and structural timber
7 Cut to maximize radial faces

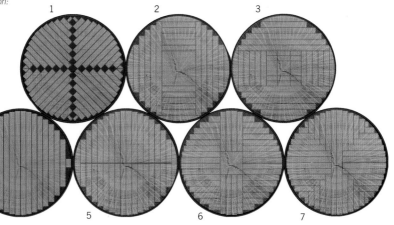

1 2 3

4 5 6 7

CUPPING

Crown-cut boards often cup away from the curve of the rings as they dry, with the contrasting diameter of the rings on either side of the plank contracting at different rates. They flatten again in moist conditions.

TWISTING AND BOWING

When boards have been badly cut, poorly stacked for drying or comprise spiraling or interlocking grain, they may twist and bow along their length. Bowing can often be the result of poor storage or stacking.

CHECKING AND SPLITTING

Small cracks occur if the surface of a board dries too fast. This is also the cause of end splits, but these are more difficult to prevent and are very common. Cracks and defects within a board may have happened during growth and are unavoidable.

SHAKES

These cracks occur within the tree, usually with one major crack working its way from the heart outward, but others can also appear.

COMMON DEFECTS IN WOOD

The woodworker who wants an easy life chooses straight-grained boards that are referred to as clean, or free from knots and defects that can weaken wood and be difficult to cut or plane. There is nothing worse than preparing lumber in the workshop, only to discover a large knot just where you want to cut a joint.

Well-managed forests produce straight, healthy trees with few knots, diseases or other defects. Many woodworkers enjoy the challenge of working with defects and believe that such features bring character to a project and reflect a more organic approach to forestry. Indeed, some defective wood is in such short supply and high demand that it is available only as veneer.

HIDDEN SECRETS

Cutting and surfacing boards reveals all manner of patterns and defects in the wood beneath. It is only after boards have been planed that the contrast between quartersawn and plain-sawn surfaces becomes apparent.

❶ Looking at the quartersawn face of this pau rosa (*Aniba duckei*) board you'd be forgiven for considering it a straight-grained lumber, but the edge reveals the wildness of the grain.

❷ The black stripes are a feature of tigerwood (*Lovoa trichilioides*), which is often referred to as African walnut. Notice how they run along the face and then across the edge.

❸ European plane (*Platanus hybrida*) is far from the only species to reveal the mottled patterning known as lacewood on quartersawn surfaces. Here the same rays are shown on the edge of a piece of European elm (*Ulmus procera*).

BURLS

Wounds to a tree's skin sometimes transform themselves into burls, made from hard, swirling scar tissue that is highly valued by turners and carvers, and for veneer. The interlocking grain makes burls very difficult to use for making furniture, and with gaps between the swirls, they are not always very strong.

KNOTS

Lumber is often graded by the frequency of knots: these weaken a board and make it difficult to work. They also tend to ooze sap or resin, and should normally be sealed with a knot sealer, usually made from shellac.

DISEASE AND AGING

Remarkable colors and patterns may be created within diseased wood, some but not all of them undermining the lumber's strength. Spalted beech features black lines, while old oak turns a deep brown color. Some lumber can be afflicted by stains, often from poor seasoning, and care must be taken that the sticks in a stack of drying wood do not stain the boards with a chemical reaction.

RIPPLE, QUILTING AND FIGURE

Extraordinary wavy patterns can be found in some woods, particularly maple and sycamore. Surprisingly, the ripple, quilting and figured grain patterns do not greatly affect the workability of these woods. The much-prized bird's-eye maple features tiny eruptions, like very small knots.

CROTCH AND ROOT

Some specialist workers of wood use the parts other craftspeople will reject. Gunsmiths, for instance, choose the dense, interlocking grain of walnut roots for gunstocks, both for its beautiful effect and because it has the strength to take recoil. Crotch wood, produced where a large branch meets the trunk, can offer rich flaming grain and is often used for panels in cabinetmaking, while boat builders and house builders will handpick curved limbs for the ribs of a boat or for a roof truss.

❹ and ❺ The difficulty of planing a wood like zebrawood, or zebrano (*Microberlinia brazzavillensis*), is illustrated by the differing grain direction on two edges of the same board.

❻ One of the more unusual features of beli (*Paraberlinia bifoliolata*) are the tiny markings you find on its surface. Easily confused with sanding marks, they are in fact entirely natural, giving the pattern an out-of-focus look.

❼ Poor seasoning can lead to checks or splits within a board, as has happened with this English oak (*Quercus robur*) board. There's little that can be done, though some woodworkers like to make a feature of them.

❽ The medullary rays that are so prominent on quartersawn oak (*Quercus* species) boards change much less for beech (*Fagus* species). The flecks are slightly larger and more lozenge-shaped on the quartersawn edge here. Notice the V-shaped grain pattern on the face which usually indicates a plain-sawn surface.

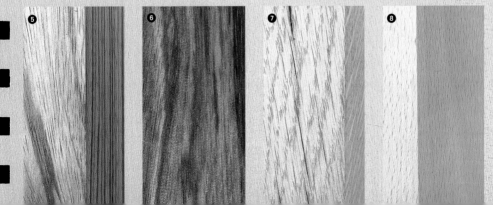

Storing Lumber

Building a stock of lumber is one of the joys of owning a workshop with space to fill. Visiting the lumber store can be a frustrating experience, taking up time and with no guarantee that you will come away with the right boards. Having a good selection at home to look through is a great advantage, and when it has been stored away for some time it somehow feels as if you are getting it for free.

Storage, though, is a challenge. The conditions must be good so that the wood is prepared for use and does not deteriorate. Knowing what you have is important, especially because rough-sawn boards are not easy to identify. Racking must be secure and stable, but easy to reach and simple to search. And then there are the offcuts, which most of us find impossible to discard in case we need exactly that species and size in the future.

KEEPING A RECORD

Holding lumberyard invoices or receipts in a folder helps when it comes to remembering what is in storage. Not all boards are bought with a project in mind, and you can soon forget exactly what you have in stock. Check off boards that have been used, and make notes on their quality and potential for future use. It is also a good idea to record how much was needed for a project, as this gradually improves your ability to draw up accurate cutting lists and bills of materials.

CONDITIONS FOR STORING LUMBER

Anyone who wants to build up a stock of lumber needs various storage solutions. Boards that are still being air-dried, in a stack with battens, should be stored outside, ideally well ventilated and protected from water and direct sunlight. The same is true of boards that have been seasoned that way and are not likely to be used for a while. A lean-to cover is perfect for this task. Use a moisture meter every six months or so to check the moisture content, and to ensure the wood is not damp.

Kiln-dried lumber will arrive at the workshop drier than air-dried boards, and it is a waste to leave it outside, as

the moisture content is likely to rise. If you don't have adequate space in the workshop, then a garage or shed is ideal for storing such boards, making sure they are well supported every 18 inches or so along their length to avoid the risk of bowing. Damp places, especially those with poor ventilation (like cellars), are unsuitable for storage as the wood is likely to deteriorate and may stain. Equally, care must be taken over storage in very hot attics, where the wood might dry too quickly and split.

Ideally, boards need final conditioning to suit the temperature and humidity of the rooms where they are

Few home woodworkers can provide the sort of ideal conditions for storing lumber that pertain in the woodyard (below left). But there's a world of difference between the neat, raised horizontal stacks of one home woodshop we visited (below) and the shove-it-in-a-corner-standing-on-its-end approach (right) of another!

likely to end up as furniture or fittings. Check the moisture content after a few weeks of conditioning in the workshop, before and after planing. If it is higher than about 12 percent, you may need final drying in the home, especially for any woods that have a tendency to move dramatically. Species and local conditions vary so much that rigid guidelines are hard to establish. It is really a case of trial and error. The ideal scenario is that the temperature and humidity of your workshop match those of the home, which is why garages attached to a house are favored by so many woodworkers for both lumber storage and woodworking.

RACKING LUMBER

Boards are best stored flat, on racking, with supports at roughly 18-inch centers to stop the lumber bending. Ideally, boards should be separated with battens, or sticks, to maintain air flow, but they can complicate matters, especially when you come to remove a piece.

Identify the boards with a color code or an abbreviation on the ends, preferably keeping species together. Many people store lumber in the eaves or under the roof, where space is otherwise often wasted. Make sure the supports are secure. Do not store lumber against external walls that might be damp. If your workshop is not very dry, wrap newly bought boards in polyethylene.

Keeping boards, especially kiln-dried boards that are ready for production, at the same moisture level in the workshop as they might expect to be in the home is a challenge. Insulation from moisture is important, as is

some warmth. Factories are likely to be centrally heated, but the home woodworker will have to rely on gentle warmth and good insulation. Garages attached to houses are good as they are usually well insulated from dampness and aren't usually too cold.

Check your stock frequently with a moisture meter, especially when you are likely to start using boards. The problems are usually most severe in winter when the contrast in relative humidity between very dry, centrally heated homes and partially heated, occasionally used workshops is at its greatest. That is when you have to be most careful with the moisture content of wood, and bring it down to somewhere around 8–9 percent. How you do this is a continual challenge for woodworkers, but some create a special insulated box within their workshops, in which they can store wood ready for use.

STORING OFFCUTS

No one wants to have to go out and buy a 12-inch length of hardwood for a jig or a new bandsaw fence when they might have it in stock already. Discarding even a nugget of rosewood is obviously a crime for woodworkers, but the decision whether to keep or discard less exotic offcuts can be more difficult to resolve. It depends, to a certain extent, upon what sort of woodworking you prefer. Boxmakers keep anything of any size; chairmakers hold on only to lengths they can use for stretchers or rails.

It takes time to recognize what is worth keeping. If you are producing small batches of repetitive designs you will quickly learn that only very specific sizes of offcut are

*Most woodworkers find offcuts **(left)**, especially of rare and exotic woods, impossible to throw away. Store them neatly in a well-ventilated pile. A good way of keeping track of what you have in your workshop is to color-code the ends of boards with a dab of latex paint **(right)**. Devise a scheme to denote different species with different colors.*

worth saving, though a quantity of offcuts of identical size or shape may inspire a new project. Woodworkers who like to experiment with ideas or prototypes will need more offcuts to feed their ever-changing requirements. Offcuts need to be stored carefully or they will soon get out of control and develop a life of their own. Racking helps, but it is best to create small compartments using vertical dividers to manage offcuts by size or species. Remember that there is only a certain quantity of offcuts you can ever need, and be careful not to waste workshop space by filling every corner with bits of wood you might never use. End-on racking works well because you can judge sections easily. Divide it into softwood and hardwood areas, or group offcuts by grain type or color.

How to Use this Book

While a book of this size cannot cover all the wood species in the world, it features the lumbers that are of value to woodworkers the world over. Some are more readily available than others, and some are beautiful enough to be worth seeking out.

Principal Woods features lumbers that are valued for their adaptability or commercial availability. In this section, too, you will find woods of great beauty, many of which, though rare and precious, are rightly considered the jewels of the lumberyard.

Secondary Woods features lumbers that are less popular with woodworkers, but still warrant

inclusion in this book. Many of these woods are of limited availability and some are of little commercial value. Others are simply of less importance or interest to the woodworker.

Special Effects features the woods in which factors such as disease, defects, grain figure or processing method can produce beautiful visual effects.

The Wood Selector, starting on page 37, is a visual index to the woods described; browse here to find the wood you want, then refer to the Wood Directory for a more detailed description.

HOW THE ENTRIES WORK

Each wood is described under a series of subheadings that provide the essential information for anyone planning to buy and use these species for woodworking. Many of the headings are self-explanatory; some require clarification, which is given below. Note that these headings have been compressed for the less-used species.

❶ BOTANICAL AND COMMON NAME
The woods are listed alphabetically by botanical name to save confusion, as several species have the same or similar common names. However, some suppliers will not know exactly what they are selling – some species can be very difficult to tell apart and come from the same part of the

world. Most-used common names are also listed under this heading.

❷ AT-A-GLANCE PROS AND CONS
Quick assessment of a wood's main qualities and defects.

❸ DESCRIPTION
Author's overview, comparing the featured wood with others.

❹ KEY CHARACTERISTICS
Type Species are identified as softwoods or hardwoods, and also indicated is whether the trees grow in tropical or temperate regions.

Other names To aid identification, the entry lists the full range of names that are commonly used to describe a particular wood. The list includes

botanical synonyms and alternative common names.

Related or similar species The related species are mostly those not listed in this book, but which you may come across in lumberyards or when you refer to other reference sources. Though a wood may have many related species, those included are closely related, but otherwise not featured. In some cases, the similar species mentioned is one with which a wood may often be confused, but to which it is not actually related.

Alternatives This heading introduces alternative species with similar characteristics.

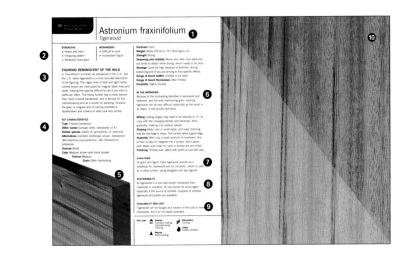

Astronomy fraxinifolium
Tigerwood

Sources This heading relates to where species are grown extensively, rather than where they might or could be grown.

Color Woods vary so greatly in color from one board to another that descriptions of color are general. However, color is the first key when you are trying to identify a species.

Texture Lumber can be coarse-grained, like oak, in which case the pores are wide and open, or it can be fine-grained, which means it is very smooth. Even or uniform texture is consistent throughout a board, whether it is coarse or fine. Uneven texture is usually the result of a contrast in the density or texture of the earlywood and latewood bands. Coarse grain is also known as open grain. Fine grain is also known as close grain.

Grain This heading describes the straightness of the grain, or whether it is wavy or interlocking. The easiest woods to use are straight-grained, but the most interesting are often wavy. Interlocking grain is often invisible until you try working it.

Hardness, weight, strength Here is described the basic characteristics of a wood, but remember that there can be wide variance in all three within a species depending on how it has been seasoned and the location where it was grown.

Seasoning and stability This heading indicates the ease and speed of seasoning, and the degree of movement once the lumber is dry. It is the latter feature that will be of much interest to woodworkers.

Wastage The amount of lumber you buy to make a project will depend on the degree of wastage you expect per board. If you buy boards ready-planed or surfaced, the wastage should be relatively low, but some species are more liable to defects and color variation that might affect how much you can obtain from a particular board.

Range of board widths and thicknesses Commonly available softwoods and hardwoods are usually available in the full range of widths and thicknesses. Species that do not grow very large may produce a smaller range of board sizes, and the supply may also be more limited for imported exotics. A restricted range may have an impact upon wastage, which is an issue when the lumber is expensive.

Durability Species vary greatly in durability, their resistance both to insects and to rot. For most woodworkers creating projects for their homes, this is not a key factor in their choice of lumbers. For those who want to use wood outside, the species that are naturally durable are identified.

There are some hardwoods that will take preservative, but only to the sapwood, so they have to be used in the round, as a log or branch. Very few hardwoods will take preservative

to the heartwood. Highlighted are species that are not durable but can take preservative. Also identified in this entry are softwood species that can be treated easily.

❺ PHOTOGRAPH OF CORNER OF BOARD
Reproduced actual size to show depth of board and detail of end-grain.

❻ IN THE WORKSHOP
Workability is one of the most important issues for a woodworker trying out a new wood. Boards with interlocking grain may be difficult to surface or mill, while others are better for shaping and profiling. The ease of gluing, nailing or screwing has a major bearing on the assembly of joints, while it is also useful to know how easily a wood can be finished, and the degree of luster that can be obtained.

❼ VARIATIONS
Different cuts of a log can reveal a varying appearance depending on grain, figure or inherent defects in the wood.

❽ SUSTAINABILITY
Indicated here is whether or not a wood is under threat, and whether sources should be checked for sustainability. Information is based on the CITES appendices and the IUCN World List of Threatened Trees, plus other data relating to endangered species. Where known, the availability of certified supplies is also given. The sustainability and certification of lumbers are subject o constant change: always check the most up-to-date information.

❾ AVAILABILITY AND COST
This depends on supply, which can fluctuate widely, so information is general, using terms such as "widely available" or "relatively expensive." Some species are obtainable only by mail order.

❿ PHOTOGRAPH OF BOARD
Photographed to show grain and figure, the board is reproduced actual size. Half of the sample is sanded but unfinished, the other half has an oil finish to bring out the beauty of the grain.

KEY USES
These are the most common uses of the lumber, and are included both to provide woodworkers with ideas and to show the lumber's wider importance in industry or as a specialist wood.

 Exterior Decking to fence posts

 Utility Packing cases, handles, utensils

 Technical From jigs to printers' blocks

 Interior Floors, cabinet-work and furniture

 Marine Boat building, from decks to masts

Joinery Includes trim and store interiors

 Decorative Turning, carving and veneers

 Luxury & leisure Sports equipment, musical instruments

 Construction General building, including timber frame

Wood Selector
Principal Woods
page 42

This section features species that are commercially available as lumber around the world, native or imported. These are the woods that are most commonly used by woodworkers.

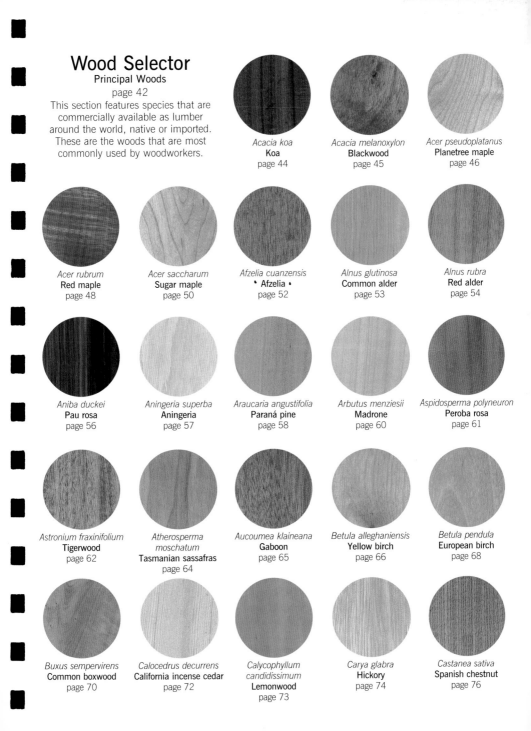

Acacia koa
Koa
page 44

Acacia melanoxylon
Blackwood
page 45

Acer pseudoplatanus
Planetree maple
page 46

Acer rubrum
Red maple
page 48

Acer saccharum
Sugar maple
page 50

Afzelia cuanzensis
• Afzelia •
page 52

Alnus glutinosa
Common alder
page 53

Alnus rubra
Red alder
page 54

Aniba duckei
Pau rosa
page 56

Aningeria superba
Aningeria
page 57

Araucaria angustifolia
Paraná pine
page 58

Arbutus menziesii
Madrone
page 60

Aspidosperma polyneuron
Peroba rosa
page 61

Astronium fraxinifolium
Tigerwood
page 62

Atherosperma moschatum
Tasmanian sassafras
page 64

Aucoumea klaineana
Gaboon
page 65

Betula alleghaniensis
Yellow birch
page 66

Betula pendula
European birch
page 68

Buxus sempervirens
Common boxwood
page 70

Calocedrus decurrens
California incense cedar
page 72

Calycophyllum candidissimum
Lemonwood
page 73

Carya glabra
Hickory
page 74

Castanea sativa
Spanish chestnut
page 76

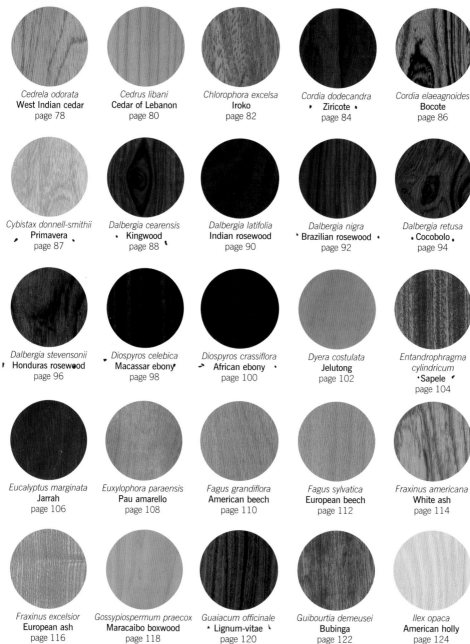

Cedrela odorata
West Indian cedar
page 78

Cedrus libani
Cedar of Lebanon
page 80

Chlorophora excelsa
Iroko
page 82

Cordia dodecandra
• Ziricote •
page 84

Cordia elaeagnoides
Bocote
page 86

Cybistax donnell-smithii
Primavera
page 87

Dalbergia cearensis
• Kingwood •
page 88

Dalbergia latifolia
Indian rosewood
page 90

Dalbergia nigra
Brazilian rosewood •
page 92

Dalbergia retusa
• Cocobolo •
page 94

Dalbergia stevensonii
Honduras rosewood
page 96

Diospyros celebica
Macassar ebony
page 98

Diospyros crassiflora
African ebony •
page 100

Dyera costulata
Jelutong
page 102

Entandrophragma cylindricum
•Sapele •
page 104

Eucalyptus marginata
Jarrah
page 106

Euxylophora paraensis
Pau amarello
page 108

Fagus grandiflora
American beech
page 110

Fagus sylvatica
European beech
page 112

Fraxinus americana
White ash
page 114

Fraxinus excelsior
European ash
page 116

Gossypiospermum praecox
Maracaibo boxwood
page 118

Guaiacum officinale
• Lignum-vitae •
page 120

Guibourtia demeusei
Bubinga
page 122

Ilex opaca
American holly
page 124

Juglans cinerea
Butternut
page 125

Juglans nigra
• **Black walnut** •
page 126

Juglans regia
• **English walnut** •
page 128

Kunzea ericoides
Kunzea
page 130

Laburnum anagyroides
Laburnum
page 131

Larix decidua
European larch
page 132

Larix occidentalis
Western larch
page 133

Liriodendron tulipifera
Tuliptree
page 134

Lovoa trichilioides
African tigerwood
page 136

Magnolia grandifolia
Southern magnolia
page 138

Malus sylvestris
Apple
page 139

Metopium brownii
Chechen
page 140

Microberlinia brazzavillensis
Zebrawood
page 142

Millettia laurentii
• **Wenge** •
page 144

Nothofagus cunninghamii
Tasmanian myrtle
page 146

Nothofagus menziesii
**New Zealand
silver beech**
page 147

Ochroma pyramidale
Balsa wood
page 148

Ocotea rodiaei
Greenheart
page 150

Paraberlinia bifoliolata
Beli
page 152

Paratecoma peroba
White peroba
page 153

Peltogyne species
Purpleheart
page 154

Pericopsis elata
Afrormosia
page 156

Picea sitchensis
Sitka spruce
page 158

Pinus monticola
Western white pine
page 159

Pinus palustris
Longleaf pine
page 160

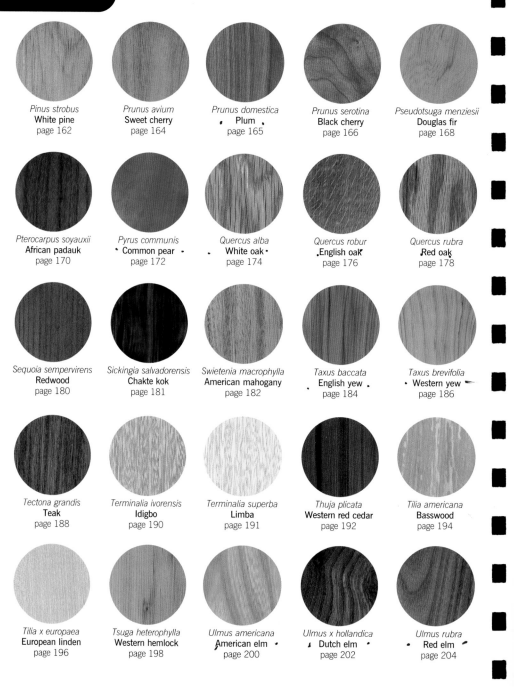

Pinus strobus
White pine
page 162

Prunus avium
Sweet cherry
page 164

Prunus domestica
Plum
page 165

Prunus serotina
Black cherry
page 166

Pseudotsuga menziesii
Douglas fir
page 168

Pterocarpus soyauxii
African padauk
page 170

Pyrus communis
Common pear
page 172

Quercus alba
White oak
page 174

Quercus robur
English oak
page 176

Quercus rubra
Red oak
page 178

Sequoia sempervirens
Redwood
page 180

Sickingia salvadorensis
Chakte kok
page 181

Swietenia macrophylla
American mahogany
page 182

Taxus baccata
English yew
page 184

Taxus brevifolia
Western yew
page 186

Tectona grandis
Teak
page 188

Terminalia ivorensis
Idigbo
page 190

Terminalia superba
Limba
page 191

Thuja plicata
Western red cedar
page 192

Tilia americana
Basswood
page 194

Tilia x europaea
European linden
page 196

Tsuga heterophylla
Western hemlock
page 198

Ulmus americana
American elm
page 200

Ulmus x hollandica
Dutch elm
page 202

Ulmus rubra
Red elm
page 204

Secondary Woods
page 206
This section contains woods that are less frequently or widely available or those that are of less importance to the woodworker.

Acanthopanax ricinofolius
Castor aralia
page 208

Aesculus hippocastanum
Horse chestnut
page 209

Brosimum paraense
Bloodwood
page 210

Caesalpinia echinata
Brazilwood
page 211

Cedrela toona
Australian red cedar
page 212

Chloroxylon swietenia
Ceylon satinwood
page 213

Dalbergia frutescens
Brazilian tulipwood
page 214

Dracontomelon dao
Paldao
page 215

Endiandra palmerstonii
Queensland walnut
page 216

Entandrophragma utile
Utile
page 217

Eucalyptus gomphocephala
Tuart
page 218

Khaya ivorensis
African mahogany
page 219

Marmaroxylon racemosum
Marblewood
page 220

Millettia stuhlmannii
Panga panga
page 221

Pinus ponderosa
Ponderosa pine
page 222

Populus species
Poplar
page 223

Pterocarpus dalbergioides
Andaman padauk
page 224

Salix alba
White willow
page 225

Swietenia mahogani
Cuban mahogany
page 226

Tieghemella heckelii
Makoré
page 227

Triplochiton scleroxylon
Obeche
page 228

Turreanthus africanus
Avodire
page 229

Special Effects
page 230
Woods in which factors such as disease, defects, grain figure or processing can produce beautiful visual effects.

Diseased wood
page 232

Figured wood
page 234

Burls
page 242

Quartersawn
page 246

PRINCIPAL WOODS

Across the world, from West Africa to New England, woodworkers choose lumber by what is available locally, creating pieces that are geographically unique. Lumberyards across a continent display subtle distinctions, with varying ranges of boards on display. However, there are also species that defy oceans and borders, and are recognized and used worldwide. The species featured in this section may be easier to acquire in one country than another, but as a group they represent a portfolio of the world's classic woods, which any keen woodworker will want to sample.

Acacia koa
Koa

STRENGTHS
- Substitute for teak
- Stable and strong

WEAKNESSES
- Interlocking grain
- Expensive

DECORATIVE HARDWOOD FROM THE HAWAIIAN ISLANDS

Koa is surprisingly hard for its moderate weight, and it takes shocks well. It is stable and relatively easy to use, though it has some interlocking grain, and working across the end-grain is said to be hard going. It is now considered the best lumber from Hawaii and is used in the making of musical instruments, particularly ukuleles, and fine furniture. In terms of color, texture and grain, it bears some resemblance to teak (*Tectona grandis*).

KEY CHARACTERISTICS

Type Tropical hardwood
Other names Hawaiian mahogany, koa-ka
Similar species *A. koaia*, which has been listed as vulnerable and is a small, gnarled tree that is found only in small numbers.
Sources Hawaiian Islands
Color Varying bands of bright, light brown or almost gold through cream, tan and mid-brown, to thin darker lines of red, brown or black
Texture Medium and even
Grain Straight or wavy, but can be interlocking
Hardness Hard, with a high luster
Weight Medium to heavy (41 lb./cu. ft.) (660 kg/cu. m)

AVAILABILITY AND SUSTAINABILITY

Koa has not been listed as endangered, but is likely to be relatively expensive. It is available only from specialist retailers of exotic hardwoods.

Key uses

Interior
Fine furniture
Cabinetmaking

Luxury & leisure
Musical instruments

Joinery
Quality interior trim

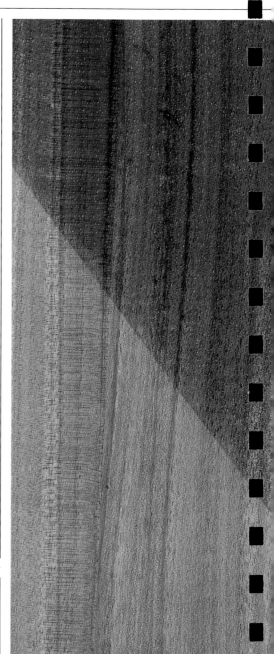

Acacia melanoxylon
Blackwood

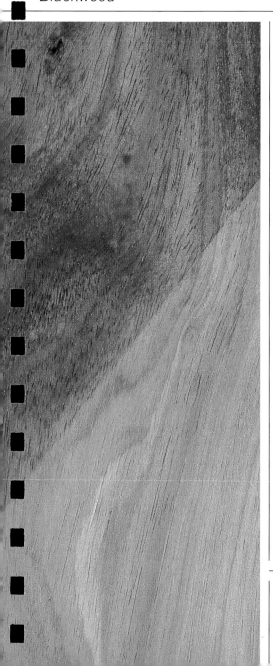

STRENGTHS
- Substitute for mahogany
- Some figured wood

WEAKNESSES
- Hard to work
- Gluing variable

MAHOGANY-STYLE LUMBER WITH WANDERING GRAIN

This is not a particularly nice lumber to work, having a wavy and interlocking grain, but the effect can be dramatic. Blackwood has some of the color of American mahogany (*Swietenia macrophylla*) but more variation in patterning and tone, though it is reported to display some fiddleback figure. Make sure you experiment with glue before assembly, and you may need to reduce cutter angles to cope with the meandering grain. However, the lumber will polish well.

KEY CHARACTERISTICS
Type Temperate hardwood
Other names Tasmanian blackwood, Australian blackwood
Similar species Black wattle (*A. mearnsii*)
Sources Australia
Color Reddish brown, with some lighter, almost golden streaks and other dark brown bands
Texture Medium
Grain Straight in some places; elsewhere wildly wavy or interlocked
Hardness Medium
Weight Medium to heavy (41 lb./cu. ft.) (660 kg/cu. m)

AVAILABILITY AND SUSTAINABILITY
Blackwood can be bought from yards specializing in exotics, and is a little more expensive than mahogany. It is not listed as endangered.

Key uses

Interior
Quality furniture

Joinery
Store interiors
Interior trim

Luxury & leisure
Gunstocks

Decorative
Turning

Acer pseudoplatanus
Planetree maple

STRENGTHS
- Inexpensive
- Even, fine texture
- Subtle figure

WEAKNESSES
- Bland
- Softer than other pale woods

SOFT *ACER*, LACKING LINES OF DISTINCTION

In many ways, planetree maple resembles its cousin sugar maple (*A. saccharum*), except that the latewood lines are less distinct and the lumber is softer in the European species. Planetree maple, which is superb to turn and useful for furniture and interior trim, has a subtle, shimmering lacewood on some quartersawn edges or faces, but it is inconsistent and evident only when the grain lies at a particular angle.

KEY CHARACTERISTICS

Type Temperate hardwood
Other names European sycamore, sycamore maple
Alternatives Butternut (*Juglans cinerea*), American whitewood (*Liriodendron tulipifera*), sycamore (*Platanus occidentalis*)
Sources Europe and Western Asia
Color Cream-white
Texture Fine and even
Grain Wavy or straight
Hardness Medium
Weight Medium (38 lb./cu. ft.) (610 kg/cu. m)
Strength Bends well but not particularly strong

Seasoning and stability Can stain if seasoned too slowly, with pink-brown coloring. Moves moderately after assembly.
Wastage Low; not much sapwood, and few defects, though staining can be an issue.
Range of board widths Good
Range of board thicknesses Good; thick boards are available.
Durability Poor; subject to rot and insect damage.

IN THE WORKSHOP

Planetree maple is not commonly used by furniture makers because it lacks the hardness and distinctive grain of sugar maple. But the workability of the lumber cannot be faulted. It is beautiful to turn, with long shavings flying from the chisel edge, and easy to use with machine or hand tools. Its fine texture finishes well.

Milling Good; tends not to chip or tear, though that can happen on figured patches. Dull tools can easily burn the surface.
Shaping Takes a good edge, but remember that it can burn.
Assembly Good; glues well, but be careful not to crush it.
Finishing Produces a lovely luster, though never quite as high as with sugar maple. Takes stain and paint very well.

VARIATIONS

The rippled, figured and fiddleback cuts are often used as veneer, sometimes pre-stained, for high-quality joinery, cabinetmaking and interior design. Silver-gray veneer is known as harewood, and weathered sycamore is also available after steaming.

SUSTAINABILITY

You may be able to find certified lumber; it is perfectly acceptable to use non-certified wood.

AVAILABILITY AND COST

It grows widely and easily across Europe. This wood is not widely available, though in Europe it is relatively easy to obtain from specialist suppliers. It is not a primary lumber, and is one of the cheaper hardwoods.

Key uses

Interior
Furniture making
Flooring

Joinery
General joinery
Interior trim

Decorative
Veneer for cabinetmaking
Turning

Utility
Kitchen utensils

Acer rubrum
Red maple

STRENGTHS
- Attractive grain pattern
- Inexpensive and readily available
- Easy to work
- Good color

WEAKNESSES
- Some small knots and defects
- Prone to blue staining during seasoning

NATIVE HARDWOOD
It is easy to be fooled into thinking red, or soft, maple is exactly that, and many woodworkers mistakenly favor sugar, or hard, maple (*A. saccharum*). In reality soft maple is only slightly softer than hard maple, and it has a better color and a more interesting grain pattern. It is often known as red maple, named for the color of the leaves on what can be a big tree.

KEY CHARACTERISTICS
Type Temperate hardwood
Other names Soft maple, scarlet maple, swamp maple, water maple
Similar species Silver maple (*A. saccharinum*), bigleaf maple (*A. macrophyllum*)
Alternatives Red elm (*Ulmus rubra*)
Sources Eastern seaboard of North America
Color Pale brown or beige-cream, with slight pink or gray hues
Texture Fine and even
Grain Straight, with some wave, but of consistent hardness
Hardness Medium-hard

Weight Medium (39 lb./cu. ft.) (620 kg/cu. m); the related species tend to be lighter.
Strength Moderate, but bends well
Seasoning and stability Slow but easy to season; little movement once dry.
Wastage Watch out for blue staining that can occur during seasoning, and there will be a few small knots and defects, but generally wastage should be low.
Range of board widths Very good
Range of board thicknesses Very good
Durability Poor

IN THE WORKSHOP
Because it is slightly softer, red maple is easier to work than sugar maple, but it is still hard enough to be an excellent lumber for most woodworking tasks.

Milling Planes very well, to a smooth surface. The texture is fine and even.
Shaping Takes a sharp edge and is easy to cut.
Assembly Take care when gluing – experiment first. Nails and screws should grip well without splitting, but proceed carefully.
Finishing Does not have the luster of sugar maple, but is fine enough not to require the use of fillers. Generally it finishes well.

VARIATIONS
Plain-sawn faces often display marvelous wandering lines reminiscent of the contours on a map. Quartersawn sides have slightly wavy lines and a faint mottled effect from the medullary rays. Many special effects are available.

SUSTAINABILITY
There is plenty of certified red maple available.

AVAILABILITY AND COST
It is plentiful, and often unnecessarily disregarded because woodworkers assume it is softer than it is, which is a pity as the reddish hue is interesting and the lumber is easy to use. It is economical to use.

Key uses

Interior Furniture making Flooring

Joinery Interior trim Paneling

Utility Handles

Luxury & leisure Musical instruments

Acer saccharum
Sugar maple

STRENGTHS
- Hard, strong and heavy
- Distinctive figure
- Even, fine texture

WEAKNESSES
- Unforgiving on tools

HARD BY NAME, HARD BY NATURE
The fine, even texture of sugar, or hard, maple and its high luster make this North American hardwood a popular species for furniture making and interior trim, particularly for kitchens. Tools may suffer, but the wood's crisp lines are ideal for contemporary designs, and it is strong, heavy, hard and stable. All these qualities make it an ideal lumber for flooring.

KEY CHARACTERISTICS
Type Temperate hardwood
Other names Rock maple, hard maple
Alternatives Beech woods (*Fagus* species), paper birch (*Betula papyrifera*)
Sources North America
Color Pale, darkening toward the heart and with distinct red-brown latewood lines
Texture Even and fine
Grain Straight to wavy
Hardness Hard
Weight Medium to heavy (46 lb./cu. ft.) (740 kg/cu. m)
Strength Strong
Seasoning and stability Slow to season, but moderately stable once dry

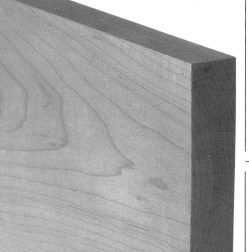

Wastage Little
Range of board widths Good
Range of board thicknesses Good
Durability Poor durability outside, with some susceptibility to insect damage

IN THE WORKSHOP
You cannot help but notice the weight and density of sugar maple, and its hardness is tough on tool edges. As a result it can be dusty to work, but it has a superb luster. Because it is so heavy and hard, it's an excellent choice for fine furniture.

Milling Planes and cuts beautifully, with minimal chipping.
Shaping Profiles can be routed sharply, and the lumber takes a good edge.
Assembly Glues well, and does not move very much, so should cause few problems. Its weight means that it tends to be used for the frames of furniture rather than the panels.
Finishing Finishes to a superb luster. Wax will not sink far into the grain, so you may be better off building up a surface finish with polish or varnish.

VARIATIONS
Maple is often cut into veneers. Variations in both the solid wood and the veneer include bird's-eye maple with its distinctive explosions of pith, and various quilted, rippled and figured maples. Such veneers are ideal for panels.

SUSTAINABILITY
Uncertified sugar maple is safe to use.

AVAILABILITY AND COST
Certified sugar maple is readily available and is moderately priced.

Key uses

🏠 **Interior**
Furniture making
Flooring

🪵 **Decorative**
Turning

⌐ **Joinery**
Interior trim

◈ **Utility**
Butchers' blocks

Afzelia cuanzensis
Afzelia

STRENGTHS
- Very stable
- Color of the best mahogany

WEAKNESSES
- Coarse texture
- Dulls tools

COARSE ALTERNATIVE TO REAL MAHOGANY

As one of the many woods that is used to imitate mahogany, afzelia is often used as an umbrella name for all the related species. It is relatively coarse in texture, and not easy to use as it can dull tool edges quickly and has some interlocking grain. It has very open pores, and however diligently you sand, more will appear, so the surface needs to be filled for a traditional perfectly smooth finish. There is little grain patterning, but afzelia's real strength is that it is very similar in color to the best mahogany (*Swietenia mahogani* or *S. macrophylla*).

KEY CHARACTERISTICS
Type Tropical hardwood
Other names Chanfuta, pod-mahogany, mahogany bean, chanfuti, peulmahonia, mkehli, makoli
Related species *A. bipindensis*, *A. pachyloba*, *A. africana*
Sources Across sub-Saharan Africa
Color Mid-reddish brown
Texture Coarse, but uniform
Grain Straight, but also interlocking
Hardness Medium
Weight Heavy (51 lb./cu. ft.) (820 kg/cu. m)

AVAILABILITY AND SUSTAINABILITY
Although *A. cuanzensis* is not listed as endangered, related species are counted as vulnerable to extinction, and it may be very difficult to identify which you are buying. Afzelia is not widely available, but should not be too expensive. There have been reports of supplies from sustainable sources, but there is little evidence of certified stock.

Key uses **Interior**
Furniture

 Joinery
General joinery
Interior trim

Alnus glutinosa
Common alder

STRENGTHS
- Stable
- Straight-grained
- Economical

WEAKNESSES
- Some small defects
- Fibrous
- Only small sizes available

UTILITY LUMBER WITH PINK HUE

Common alder is one of those versatile lumbers that are not often used by hobby woodworkers, or even professional furniture makers, but it is employed in mass production and joinery. It seasons well, is stable in use and is neither strong nor weak. Though alder is relatively easy to work, its fibrous nature means that you will need to keep cutters sharp to shape a good profile or edge. It stains and finishes well, but not to a high luster. As a result it tends to be used for utility purposes, particularly turned items, because it turns well. Alder tends not to grow very large, so board widths may be limited, and there is a risk of cupping.

KEY CHARACTERISTICS

Type Temperate hardwood
Other names Black alder, gray alder, European alder
Related species *A. incana*
Sources Europe, but also North Africa and Japan
Color Pale pinky cream, at times almost white, but sometimes a light red-brown
Texture Fine and uniform
Grain Straight
Hardness Medium
Weight Medium (33 lb./cu. ft.) (530 kg/cu. m)

AVAILABILITY AND SUSTAINABILITY

Common alder is not widely available, but it is inexpensive and not threatened.

Key uses

Utility
Handles
Utensils

 Luxury & leisure
Toys

Joinery
Store interiors
Interior trim

Alnus rubra
Red alder

STRENGTHS	WEAKNESSES
• Plentiful and economical	• Bland
• Stable and consistent	• Soft
• Easy to work, versatile	• Lacks luster

UTILITY LUMBER WITH MANY USES

Red alder has become an important utility lumber. Stable, economical and plentiful, it is used as a core for veneer and in the solid for mass-produced furniture. The inner bark turns a reddish orange when exposed to the air, hence the name. There are many alder species in North America, but red alder is one of only two that are available commercially, the other being white alder (*A. rhombifolia*).

KEY CHARACTERISTICS

Type Temperate hardwood
Other names Oregon alder, Pacific Coast alder, western alder
Similar species Seaside alder (*A. maritima*), Arizona alder (*A. oblongifolia*), white alder (*A. rhombifolia*), speckled alder (*A. rugosa*), hazel alder (*A. serrulata*), sitka alder (*A. sinuata*), mountain alder (*A. tenuifolia*)
Alternatives Birch (*Betula* species), hickory (*Carya* species), beech (*Fagus* species), aspen (*Populus* species)
Sources Pacific coast of North America from Alaska to California
Color Very pale to almost white when cut, with no clear sapwood. Darkens to yellowish red or light brown.

Texture Fine and even
Grain Generally straight and inconspicuous
Hardness Soft
Weight Light (28 lb./cu. ft.) (450 kg/cu. m)
Strength Moderate, but good for such a light lumber
Seasoning and stability Easy to season quickly, and very stable once dry
Wastage Low
Range of board widths Good
Range of board thicknesses Good
Durability Poor durability in the ground, but better in water. Prone to some insect attack.

IN THE WORKSHOP

Though red alder is easy to work and stable, the lumber is relatively soft and you need sharp tools to get a smooth surface. Because it is so stable it is often used as a core for mahogany or walnut veneer. The dust is reported by some woodworkers to cause some skin irritation.

Milling Cutting and planing is good, but blades must be sharp or the fibers will tear.
Shaping The softness of red alder means you will not achieve the best edges, but it is ideal for utility furniture or joinery.
Assembly Glues effectively, but does not hold screws or nails very well.
Finishing Takes stains well to imitate other species, but the luster is not very high.

VARIATIONS

Often cut for veneer.

SUSTAINABILITY

Red alder is fast growing and widely grown, so there should be no issues regarding sustainability. You can find certified red alder, but specifying it is perhaps not as important as for other species.

AVAILABILITY AND COST

Widely available and relatively inexpensive.

Key uses	Interior		Decorative
	Furniture		Carving
			Turning
			Core for veneering

Aniba duckei
Pau rosa

STRENGTHS
- Hard, strong and durable
- Relatively easy to use
- Interesting grain pattern

WEAKNESSES
- Possibly endangered
- Limited supply
- Likely to be inconsistent

ROSEWOOD SUBSTITUTE WITH PINK COLORS

Pau rosa is a name associated with many other species, including Brazilian rosewood (*Dalbergia nigra*), Brazilian tulipwood (*D. frutescens*) and various laurels (*Laurus* species). It is also the name of an evenly pink lumber from Mozambique. Studying the end-grain of this pau rosa reveals a spectrum of golds, reds, purples and dark browns. With a straight grain that gently waves, pau rosa has an even but coarse texture and inconsistent color. It is very much in the rosewood style of lumber, with swirling shapes on crown-cut faces or edges, and clear lines of varying width on quartersawn cuts.

KEY CHARACTERISTICS

Type Tropical hardwood
Other names Brazilian louro, louro rosa
Similar species *A. rosaeodora*
Sources Brazil
Color Varies, from gold to red to purple and very dark brown
Texture Even but medium-coarse
Grain Straight with slight wave
Hardness Hard
Weight Heavy (51 lb./cu. ft.) (820 kg/cu. m)

AVAILABILITY AND SUSTAINABILITY

Some lists show *A. duckei* as being endangered. We have found no certified supplies. It may only be available at specialist yards, but is unlikely to be expensive.
A. rosaeodora is thought to be endangered in most South American countries, because of rosewood oil extraction.

Key uses

 Interior Furniture making Flooring

 Decorative Veneer Turning

Utility Tool handles

Aningeria superba
Aningeria

STRENGTHS
- Even texture
- Easily stained
- Can have mottled figure

WEAKNESSES
- Generally bland
- Can crack
- Abrasive

RELIABLE SUBSTITUTE FOR CLASSIC SPECIES

A relatively uninteresting lumber, aningeria is generally used for furniture and stained to reproduce walnut, cherry or oak. Quartersawn boards, especially those with some mottled figuring, can be dramatic on their own and worth using for tabletops or paneling. It is generally easy to work, though is reputed to be slightly abrasive and might dull tool edges quickly. It also has a tendency to crack and is only moderately strong, and not especially good for bending. However, it seasons well and quickly, and moves very little once dry.

KEY CHARACTERISTICS
Type Tropical hardwood
Other names Anigre, anegré
Related species *A. robusta*, *A. altissima*, *A. adolfi-friederici*, *A. pseudo-racemosa*
Sources Africa
Color Pale brown or tan with a creamy or pinkish hue
Texture Medium to coarse, but very even
Grain Generally straight, but some figuring or mottling across the grain. Growth rings can be seen on quartered surfaces.
Hardness Medium to hard
Weight Medium (c. 33 lb./cu. ft.) (530 kg/cu. m)

AVAILABILITY AND SUSTAINABILITY
Aningeria is not widely available but is sold around the world as veneer for paneling, cabinets and furniture. There are no obvious sources of certified lumber, and the most authoritative lists of endangered species do not mention it.

Key uses ▶ **Joinery**
Interior trim
General joinery
Plywood

 Decorative
Veneer for cabinets

Araucaria angustifolia
Paraná pine

STRENGTHS
- Unusual coloring
- Close, dense grain makes working easy
- Often supplied planed
- Low wastage
- Less expensive than most hardwoods

WEAKNESSES
- Not strong
- More expensive than most softwoods
- Interesting color dulls with age
- Can move dramatically

DENSE SOFTWOOD WITH UNUSUAL COLORING

Paraná pine is one of the most attractive of woods for home improvers who want to take their first steps in woodwork. Very dense for a softwood, it is easy to use and has more depth of color than the Pinaceae pines.

KEY CHARACTERISTICS

Type Tropical softwood
Other names Brazilian pine
Alternatives Peroba rosa (*Aspidosperma polyneuron*), yellow birch (*Betula alleghaniensis*)
Sources Argentina, Brazil, Paraguay
Color Largely honey colored, but with streaks of dark brown and even red, though the latter fade with time.
Texture Even and smooth; takes a precise edge
Grain Very close-grained, with no obvious growth rings, making it consistent and easy to use
Hardness Hard for a softwood, but will bruise

Weight Varies greatly, but generally medium (30–40 lb./cu. ft.) (480–640 kg/cu. m)
Strength Only moderate bending and crushing strength, and not very resistant to shock. Tends to be used in thicker sections for shelves.
Seasoning and stability Difficult to season, and can split badly in the darker areas, so check boards carefully before buying. Watch out also for bent boards.
Wastage Can be some sapwood, but wastage is relatively low unless the board is split.
Range of board widths Reasonable, but beware of cupping on wider boards.
Range of board thicknesses Moderate
Durability Poor durability outside, and vulnerable to some insects. Can be reasonably well protected with preservative.

IN THE WORKSHOP

For anyone who has only worked with inexpensive softwoods, parana pine will be a luxury. The grain is even and straight, and there is little risk of chipping.

Milling Easy, and lumber is usually supplied S4S. Cupping is a problem.
Shaping Takes an edge very well and is easy to work with hand tools and machines. Does not dull tools.
Assembly Forgiving. Joints can be cut easily and accurately. Glues well.
Finishing Takes any finish and produces a deep luster. But beware of bruising: parana pine may have the texture of a hardwood, but it is relatively soft.

SUSTAINABILITY

Paraná pine is one of very few tropical softwoods. It is listed as CITES Appendix I and vulnerable by IUCN, and there is a risk of illegal logging.

AVAILABILITY AND COST

Widely available through contractor's suppliers as the top end of the softwood market. It is usually supplied planed with straight edges rather than sawn, so the cost is high for a softwood, but medium compared to a hardwood.

Key uses	Interior	Joinery
	Basic furniture and cabinetmaking	Joinery Store interiors

Arbutus menziesii
Madrone

STRENGTHS
- Subtle color and pattern
- Smooth and even texture

WEAKNESSES
- Unstable and difficult to season
- Dulls machine tools

LITTLE-USED HARDWOOD RESEMBLING CHERRY

Madrone has some similarity to a fruitwood, and is known in the United Kingdom as the strawberry tree. It is like a combination of pearwood and black cherry, being a pinkish brown with subtle, straight grain patterning, though the coloring tends to be irregular. An evergreen hardwood, it grows along the northwest coast of North America. Madrone finishes well and is relatively easy to work, though it is reported to dull machine blades quickly, and some woodworkers say it is difficult to glue. It does not season well and is not particularly stable once dry.

KEY CHARACTERISTICS
Type Temperate hardwood
Other names Madrona, Pacific madrone, madroño, bullbay, big laurel, bat tree, arbuti tree, strawberry tree (U.K.)
Related species *A. procera*, *A. unedo* (strawberry madrone), *A. crispo*, *A. salicifolia*, *A. serratifolia*, *A. vulgaris*
Sources Northwest North America
Color Pink-brown with paler streaks
Texture Fine and even, and very smooth to touch
Grain Generally straight
Hardness Medium
Weight Medium to heavy (48 lb./cu. ft.) (770 kg/cu. m)

AVAILABILITY AND SUSTAINABILITY
Not widely available, nor seemingly endangered, as it is not of great commercial value. The burls are valued for making pipes and veneer.

Key uses

 Interior Furniture

Luxury & leisure Musical instruments

 Decorative Turning Inlay and veneer

Aspidosperma polyneuron
Peroba rosa

STRENGTHS
- Distinctive color
- Smooth, fine and even texture
- Generally straight grain

WEAKNESSES
- Can be weak and brittle
- Darker streaks can be a nuisance

DISTINCTIVELY COLORED HARDWOOD

Like so many tropical hardwoods, peroba rosa is a joy to use when the grain is straight, but a devil when it is interlocking. More often than not, though, this is an easy wood to work, with a creamy texture and only a slight risk of chipping. It has a distinctive orangey color and a very smooth luster. Used for construction in Brazil, it is growing in popularity elsewhere for furniture and interior trim. This species is certainly worth trying, but be aware that within a board you are likely to encounter darker streaks that may be difficult to avoid. Peroba rosa is likely to move moderately once dry, and there is some risk of distortion during seasoning.

KEY CHARACTERISTICS

Type Tropical hardwood
Other names *A. peroba*, rosa peroba, red peroba, pink peroba, palo rosa, amargosa, amarello
Related species *A. desmanthum*, *A. australe*
Sources Brazil and other South American countries
Color Pale red or orange, with some much darker streaks
Texture Fine and even
Grain Generally straight, but some interlocking or wavy grain
Hardness Medium to hard
Weight Medium to heavy (47 lb./cu. ft.) (750 kg/cu. m)

AVAILABILITY AND SUSTAINABILITY

Peroba rosa is used extensively in Brazil and is now widely available elsewhere at a moderate price. It has been listed by the IUCN as endangered, but fortunately certified supplies are available and should be used whenever possible.

Key uses

 Interior
Furniture
Flooring

Joinery
General joinery
Interior trim

 Decorative
Turning
Veneer

Astronium fraxinifolium
Tigerwood

STRENGTHS
- Heavy and hard
- Intriguing pattern
- Relatively close grain

WEAKNESSES
- Difficult to work
- Inconsistent figure

FIGURING REMINISCENT OF THE WILD

A. fraxinifolium is known as zebrawood in the U.K., but the U.S. name tigerwood is a more accurate description of the figuring. The vague lines of dark and light honey-colored brown are interrupted by irregular black lines and spots, making this species difficult to use if you want a particular effect. The heavy lumber has a closer texture than many tropical hardwoods, and is favored for fine cabinetmaking and as a veneer for paneling. However, the grain is irregular and of varying consistency. Quartersawn and crown-cut sides look very similar.

KEY CHARACTERISTICS
Type Tropical hardwood
Other names Gonçalo alves, zebrawood (U.K.)
Similar species Jobillo (*A. graveolens*), *A. balansae*
Alternatives Cocobolo (*Dalbergia retusa*), zebrawood (*Microberlinia brazzavillensis*), beli (*Paraberlinia bifoliolata*)
Sources Brazil
Color Medium brown with black streaks
Texture Medium
Grain Often interlocking

Hardness Hard
Weight Heavy (59 lb./cu. ft.) (940 kg/cu. m)
Strength Strong
Seasoning and stability Moves very little once seasoned, but tends to distort while drying, which needs to be slow.
Wastage Could be high because of distortion during seasoning and if you are aiming to find specific effects.
Range of board widths Unlikely to be wide
Range of board thicknesses Often limited
Durability Highly durable

IN THE WORKSHOP
Because of the contrasting densities of earlywood and latewood, and the wild interlocking grain, working tigerwood can be very difficult, especially as the wood is so heavy. It will quickly dull tools.

Milling Cutting angles may need to be reduced to 15° to cope with the changing density and hardness. Work gradually, making only shallow passes.
Shaping Make cuts in small steps, and keep checking that the tool edge is sharp. The lumber takes a good edge.
Assembly With only a small amount of movement, this lumber is easy to integrate into a project, and it glues well. Make sure holes for nails or screws are pre-drilled.
Finishing Finishes well, either with polish or just with wax.

VARIATIONS
Its grain and figure make tigerwood popular as a substitute for rosewoods and for cocobolo. Jobillo is used as a utility lumber, being straighter and less figured.

SUSTAINABILITY
As tigerwood is a less well-known hardwood than rosewood or cocobolo, its use should be encouraged, especially if the source is certified. Supplies of certified tigerwood and jobillo are available.

AVAILABILITY AND COST
Tigerwood can be bought at a fraction of the cost of many rosewoods, but it is not readily available.

Key uses

Interior
Furniture making
Cabinetmaking
Flooring

Marine
Boat building

Decorative
Turning

Utility
Cutlery handles

Atherosperma moschatum
Tasmanian sassafras

STRENGTHS
- Versatile
- Easy to work
- Interesting black staining

WEAKNESSES
- Bland patterning
- Confusion regarding species

VERSATILE AUSTRALIAN SOFTWOOD THAT CAN BE BLACK OR WHITE

Sassafras is one of the most common lumbers in Australia, and is used extensively for furniture, interior trim and woodturning. The name sassafras is used for various unrelated species, including American sassafras (*Sassafras albidum*), which is prized for its flavorful root-bark. Tasmanian sassafras has some similarities to birch (*Betula* species) and alder (*Alnus* species), and is used for the same range of utility purposes. It is slightly harder and heavier than those North American species. Easy to work and finish, it is also reported to be stable. Initially tan or gray, the heartwood can turn black if it decays, and there have been reports of foresters intentionally injuring trees in order to encourage such staining.

KEY CHARACTERISTICS
Type Temperate hardwood
Other names Australian sassafras, black sassafras, white sassafras
Sources Australia
Color Pale tan or gray, with some darker staining and streaks. Decayed wood turns black.
Texture Fine and even, but slightly fibrous
Grain Straight, and hardly noticeable
Hardness Medium
Weight Medium (37 lb./cu. ft.) (590 kg/cu. m)

AVAILABILITY AND SUSTAINABILITY
Sassafras is very common in Australia, but not often imported to North America. There are no signs of sassafras being vulnerable. Blackened sassafras is likely to be more expensive than the white variety.

Key uses **Interior**
Furniture
Flooring

Joinery
Interior trim
General joinery

Decorative
Turning
Carving

Aucoumea klaineana
Gaboon

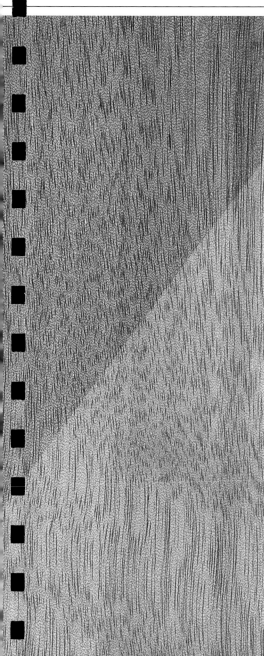

STRENGTHS
- Inexpensive

WEAKNESSES
- Interlocking grain
- Undistinguished figure
- Weak

MAHOGANY SUBSTITUTE USED MAINLY FOR PLYWOOD

Most commonly used in the production of plywood, gaboon is one of the key species for replacing true mahogany (*Swietenia macrophylla*) in reproduction furniture and for moldings. It is also used for interior trim and joinery, and in boat building. Not particularly strong or durable, it has a consistent, medium texture and variable grain that is neither very difficult to work nor very easy. Grown in Central Africa, particularly Gabon, gaboon dries well and moves moderately once seasoned.

KEY CHARACTERISTICS
Type Tropical hardwood
Sources Central Africa
Color Pinkish red heartwood with pale gray or white sapwood. It resembles true mahogany.
Texture Medium to coarse, but uniform
Grain Variable, with some straight but also wavy and interlocking
Hardness Medium
Weight Light (27 lb./cu. ft.) (430 kg/cu. m)

AVAILABILITY AND SUSTAINABILITY
Gaboon is more widely available in Europe than the United States, where West Indian cedar (*Cedrela odorata*), Santa Maria (*Calophyllum braziliensis*) or jatoba (*Hymenaea courbaril*) are more common alternatives for true mahogany. It is listed as vulnerable by IUCN, and there are concerns over its long-term status because of overexploitation.

Key uses

Joinery
Moldings and trim
General joinery
Plywood

Decorative
Veneer

Interior
Reproduction furniture

Utility
Blockboard
Packing crates

Betula alleghaniensis
Yellow birch

STRENGTHS

- Widely available and economical
- Fine and even texture
- Close-grained and easy to work

WEAKNESSES

- Considerable movement when dry
- Not durable
- Some inconsistent grain

THE BEST OF MANY AVAILABLE BIRCHES

Birch is one of the most prolific of species in North America, and there are many variations, but yellow birch is the best for woodworkers and the most commonly available. It is grown mostly in the northeast and the Great Lake states, and is used extensively for simple jobs and in the production of plywood. The distinctive smell of the lumber resonates with anyone who has used it.

KEY CHARACTERISTICS

Type Temperate hardwood
Other names *B. lutea* (synonym), gray birch, Canadian silky birch, hard birch, silver birch, swamp birch, curly birch, white birch, witch hazel
Similar species Sweet birch (*B. lenta*), paper birch (*B. papyrifera*), river birch (*B. nigra*), gray birch (*B. populifolia*)
Alternatives Beech (*Fagus grandifolia* or *F. sylvatica*)
Sources North America
Color Light reddish brown heartwood and pale sapwood
Texture Fine and even

Grain Straight
Hardness Moderate
Weight Medium to heavy (44 lb./cu. ft.) (700 kg/cu. m)
Strength Good; excellent for bending
Seasoning and stability Seasons slowly but well, and moves considerably once dry.
Wastage Moderate; some knots and sapwood
Range of board widths Good
Range of board thicknesses Good
Durability Poor; vulnerable to insect attack and decay. Heartwood cannot be preserved easily.

IN THE WORKSHOP

Birch tends to be more commonly used for utility purposes than for fine furniture, though its bending qualities make it suitable for chairmaking. The dust can be very fine, and has been known to cause skin irritation.

Milling Can tear around knots and has some dulling effect on edges.
Shaping Takes a good edge.
Assembly Can split on nailing, but holds well to screws and nails, and glues very well.
Finishing Finishes to an excellent luster and takes stain well.

VARIATIONS

Birch is often used for veneer, either sliced or rotary cut. The rotary-cut version can show distinctive growth-ring patterns.

SUSTAINABILITY

There is no threat to yellow birch.

AVAILABILITY AND COST

Widely available and inexpensive.

Key uses   **Interior** Furniture making   **Decorative** Veneer

Joinery Interior trim Plywood

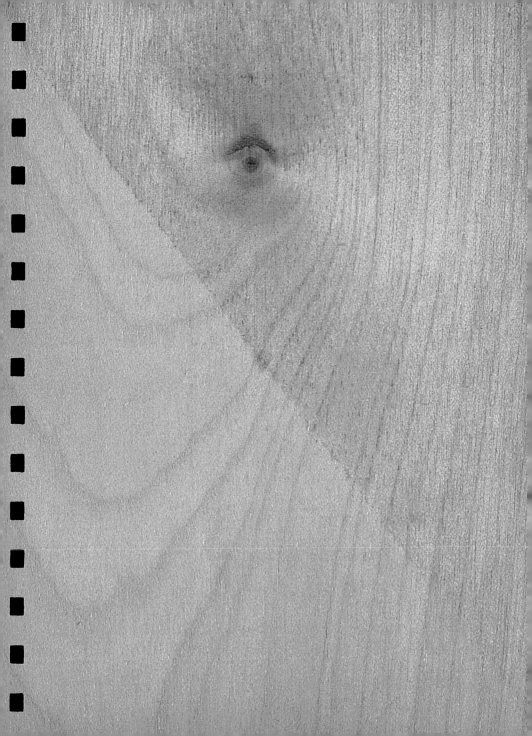

Betula pendula
European birch

STRENGTHS

- Fine, even texture
- Straight grain is easy to use
- Inexpensive and easy to season

WEAKNESSES

- Bland appearance
- Limited to smaller dimensions
- Not durable

VERSATILE UTILITY LUMBER

Used for mass-produced furniture and plywood, European birch is not regarded as an obvious choice for high-quality work. Birch tree trunks do not tend to grow very thick so boards are likely to be relatively narrow. The color and patterning are uninteresting and the lumber's good qualities are reserved for utility purposes. It is employed extensively for hidden components in joinery, and it bends well. It also takes stain well and is often used for ready-to-assemble furniture.

KEY CHARACTERISTICS

Type Temperate hardwood
Other names Many names are used for European birch to describe specific cuts or effects. These include Masur birch, Karelian birch and ice birch. The names also relate to the country of origin.
Related species *B. pubescens*, *B. alba* and *B. odorata* are often sold as European birch.
Alternatives American whitewood (*Liriodendron tulipifera*) or other birch species (*Betula* species)

Sources Europe
Color Creamy white to very pale tan
Texture Fine to medium and very uniform; good luster
Grain Straight
Hardness Medium
Weight Varies, but generally medium to heavy (37–43 lb./cu. ft.) (590–690 kg/cu. m)
Strength Good; excellent for bending.
Seasoning and stability It dries fairly rapidly with a slight tendency to warp.
Wastage Moderate
Range of board widths Limited widths as European birch is not one of the largest of trees.
Range of board thicknesses European birch is used most commonly for plywood, but some boards will be available.
Durability Poor; vulnerable to insect attack and decay. Heartwood is moderately resistant to preservative treatment.

IN THE WORKSHOP

European birch tends to be used for mass-produced rather than fine furniture. It is commonly used for plywood, but special cuts are favored as veneer (especially when stained various colors) and for turning.

Milling Birch is easy to plane and cut by hand or machine.
Shaping Birch takes a good edge for profiling and is often used for bending in mass-produced furniture.
Assembling You can glue, screw and nail birch easily.
Finishing Birch finishes well enough, though it can be a bit furry. It has a good luster and is easy to stain.

SUSTAINABILITY

There is no shortage of supply, so no real need to specify certified sources.

AVAILABILITY AND COST

European birch is more widely available as plywood than as solid boards, and is relatively inexpensive.

Key uses	Joinery	Interior
	Plywood Hidden components	Mass-produced furniture Ready-to-assemble furniture Flooring

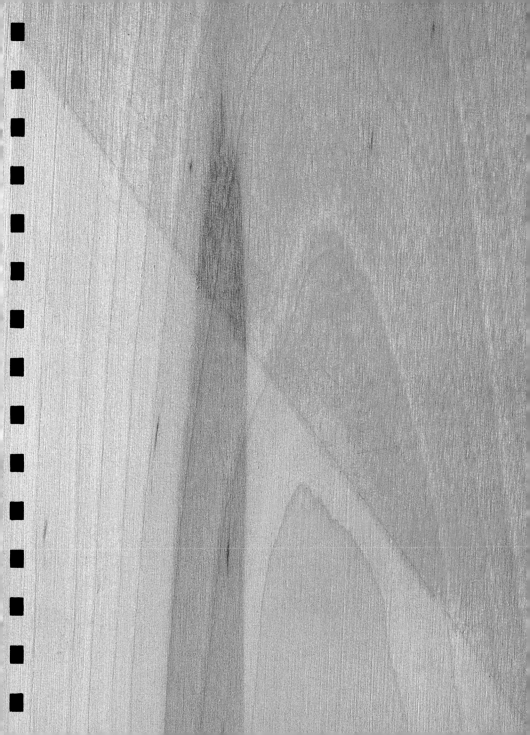

Buxus sempervirens
Common boxwood

STRENGTHS
- Hard and tough
- Dense, with close-grained, fine texture
- Warm yellow color

WEAKNESSES
- Very limited availability
- Restricted range of dimensions
- Wavy grain and a tendency to tear

HEDGING LUMBER IDEAL FOR TOOLS

You will not find many 6-inch-wide boards of common boxwood, nor panels constructed from boxwood strips. Though its smooth, close-grained texture makes it popular for decorative veneering, especially for bandings and stringing, it is used sparingly by furniture makers. Turners like its density and toolmakers favor it for mallet heads and chisel handles, as it is hard and does not split. It is often used for making chess pieces. The color can vary considerably and the grain can be difficult to use.

KEY CHARACTERISTICS
Type Temperate hardwood
Other names European boxwood
Similar species East London boxwood (*B. macowani*), Maracaibo boxwood (*Gossypiospermum praecox*)
Alternatives Jelutong (*Dyera costulata*)
Sources Grows wild as bushes and trees across Europe
Color Yellow to light brown
Texture Fine and even
Grain Straight to wavy, but small knots common
Hardness Hard
Weight Heavy (56 lb./cu. ft.) (900 kg/cu. m)

Strength Very tough
Seasoning and stability Slow to season, and tends to split at the ends if not planked, or on the surface. Small amount of movement once dry.
Wastage Relatively high as it is available only from small-diameter roundwood and has defects and sapwood.
Range of board widths Very limited
Range of board thicknesses Very limited
Durability Durable outdoors, though it is unlikely to be used in the ground; vulnerable to insect damage indoors.

IN THE WORKSHOP
It turns beautifully with the shavings streaming off the edge. Carvers like it for the creamy, dense texture, but only in small quantities because it is very difficult to assemble boards into a consistent block.

Milling Considerable risk of tearing, and you may need to use a scraper for the final smoothing.
Shaping Hard and dense, so it takes detail very well, though the wavy grain and risk of knots can make it brittle and likely to snap along its length.
Assembly Glues well. Very difficult to match boards if you are trying to assemble panels.
Finishing Takes stain well and polishes beautifully, with a superb luster.

VARIATIONS
The end-grain of common boxwood is favored for printing blocks; otherwise it is used largely for decorative inserts in cabinetry.

SUSTAINABILITY
Boxwood lumber is randomly sourced from trees and hedges that have reached maturity or need to be removed, hence its rarity. You are unlikely to find certified stock, but there is little risk to boxwood from harvesting.

AVAILABILITY AND COST
Very limited supplies. It can be expensive, and is available from specialist yards.

Key uses

Utility Tool handles

Technical Scientific instruments Engraving and printing blocks

Decorative Decorative effects in cabinetry

Luxury & leisure Musical instruments Chess pieces

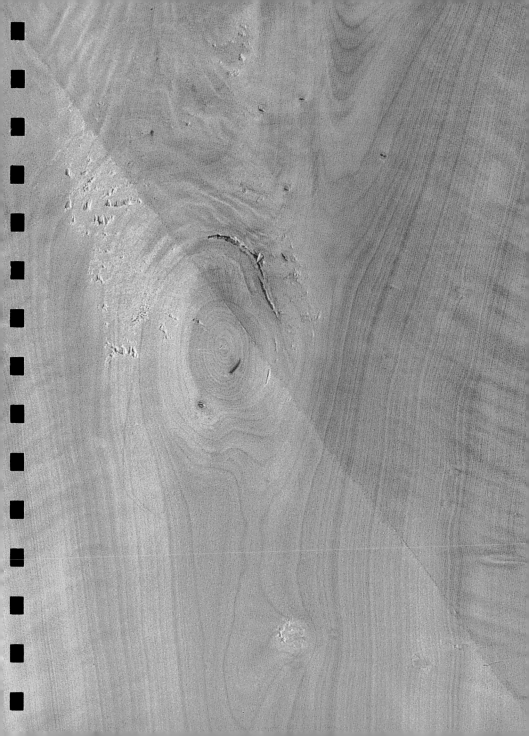

Calocedrus decurrens
California incense cedar

STRENGTHS	WEAKNESSES
• Durable	• Liable to decay
• Easy to use	• Very soft
• Aromatic	

AROMATIC AND VERY DURABLE SOFTWOOD

Though it is lightweight and soft, incense cedar is useful for its durability, straight grain and aroma. It is popular for fence posts and for making pencils, because the wood can be sharpened easily. An aromatic lumber, it is also favored by furniture makers for constructing drawers and boxes as an alternative to cedar of Lebanon (*Cedrus libani*), which is used extensively in Europe for that purpose.

KEY CHARACTERISTICS

Type Temperate softwood
Other names *Libocedrus decurrens*, incense cedar, *Heyderia decurrens*
Sources West coast of United States
Color Light brown or tan color with a slight reddish hue
Texture Fine and even
Grain Straight
Hardness Soft and often liable to decay, and not very strong. However, it is very durable.
Weight Light (26 lb./cu. ft.) (420 kg/cu. m)

AVAILABILITY AND SUSTAINABILITY

Widely available and under no threat. Incense cedar tends to be grown in mixed forests, so there should be no risk to biodiversity.

Key uses **Interior** Furniture · **Utility** Pencils · **Exterior** Posts Railroad ties · **Luxury & leisure** Toys

Calycophyllum candidissimum
Lemonwood

STRENGTHS
- Easy to work
- Fine, even texture

WEAKNESSES
- No distinctive pattern
- Not durable

OLIVE HARDWOOD WITH A TOUCH OF BOX

Lemonwood is a delight to use, being hard but straight-grained, and though the grain pattern is not particularly distinctive, the color is subtle, ranging from tan and yellow to olive. It has some of the feel of European boxwood (*Buxus sempervirens*), but with straighter grain and less variation. It is also a bit darker. Lemonwood is stable and seasons well, and is both strong and good for bending, but it is not durable. It is similar to jelutong (*Dyera costulata*), but with more character, so is popular with carvers. It is easier to work than boxwood because it does not have as many defects and knots.

KEY CHARACTERISTICS
Type Tropical hardwood
Other names Degame
Sources Central and South America, and Cuba
Color Tan to olive, with pale sapwood
Texture Fine and even
Grain Fairly straight
Hardness Hard
Weight Heavy (51 lb./cu. ft.) (820 kg/cu. m)

AVAILABILITY AND SUSTAINABILITY
Not listed as endangered but not widely available. However, lemonwood is not a favored lumber so it should be inexpensive.

Key uses

Interior
Cabinetmaking

Joinery
Interior trim

Utility
Handles

Luxury & leisure
Bows for archery
Billiard cues

Decorative
Carving
Turning

Carya glabra
Hickory

STRENGTHS
- Strong
- Bends well
- Good for handles
- Inexpensive

WEAKNESSES
- Bland
- Distorts during seasoning
- Moves after seasoning
- Difficult to work

STRONG WOOD FOR HANDLES AND SPORTS
Hickory shares some of the whippy nature of white ash (*Fraxinus americana*) and European ash (*F. excelsior*). The coloring is less consistent, with pinkish latewood and yellowish earlywood, and occasional thin, dark brown lines. This irregularity and the coarse texture mean hickory is not the first choice when looks are at a premium, but it is favored for drumsticks, fishing rods, skis, tool handles, handmade car bodies and other items that need flexibility and good shock resistance.

KEY CHARACTERISTICS
Type Temperate hardwood
Other names Pignut hickory (U.S.), broom hickory
Similar species Mockernut hickory (*C. tomentosa*), shellbark hickory (*C. laciniosa*), shagbark, red or white hickory (*C. ovata*), nutmeg hickory (*C. myristiciformis*)
Alternatives American beech (*Fagus grandifolia*), European ash (*Fraxinus excelsior*), white ash (*F. alba*), butternut (*Juglans cinerea*)
Sources Eastern North America
Color Cream to pinkish brown
Texture Coarse

Grain Straight or wavy
Hardness Hard
Weight Heavy (51 lb./cu. ft.) (820 kg/cu. m)
Strength Strong, shock resistant and bends well
Seasoning and stability Distorts during seasoning but dries quickly, with some shrinkage.
Wastage Some hickories split in seasoning, which may increase wastage, but the white sapwood is of value.
Range of board widths Good
Range of board thicknesses Good
Durability Poor; prone to pests and to rot in the ground

IN THE WORKSHOP
The irregular grain can make hickory difficult to work. The texture is coarse, so care must be taken when working, but a good finish can be achieved.

Milling Reduce the cutter angle when surfacing to reduce the risk of chipping and tearing.
Shaping Good and hard for profiling and cutting joints, but the irregular grain may affect accuracy and may catch router cutters.
Assembly Fine; plenty of give, and movement is limited once the wood is seasoned. But hickory is rarely used for panels or furniture.
Finishing May need significant sanding, but the surface is hard and a good luster can be achieved. Use stains to emphasize the open grain patterns.

VARIATIONS
Pecan (*C. illinoinensis*) is similar to the hickories, but isn't recommended for much more than utility lumber.

SUSTAINABILITY
There is no indication that hickory is under threat, and it is very unlikely to be. Certified hickory is available.

AVAILABILITY AND COST
The availability and cost of the various hickory species may vary, but prices are moderate for a hardwood, and lumber should be easy to find in a specialist yard.

Key uses

 Utility Handles for tools

 Interior Flooring

 Luxury & leisure Drumsticks Sports equipment

Decorative Veneer for paneling

Castanea sativa
Spanish chestnut

STRENGTHS
- Cheaper than European oak
- Possible straight grain
- Good figure

WEAKNESSES
- Grain can spiral
- Corrosive in contact with ferrous metals
- Doesn't season easily
- No medullary ray patterning

HARDWOOD THAT RESEMBLES OAK

Spanish chestnut is often described as poor man's oak, because it is strong and durable. However, it is neither as easy to use nor as well figured. Preferred to horse chestnut (*Aesculus hippocastanum*), Spanish chestnut has no obvious medullary rays, and plain-sawn faces resemble dark European ash (*Fraxinus excelsior*). As can be seen from the growth of the bark in the living tree, the grain is straight or spiraling, but tends not to be as interlocking as you might imagine.

KEY CHARACTERISTICS

Type Temperate hardwood
Other names European sweet chestnut, *C. vesca*
Similar species American chestnut (*C. dentata*)
Alternatives Oak (*Quercus* species), ash (*Fraxinus sylvatica* and *F. excelsior*), elm (*Ulmus hollandica* and *U. americana*)
Sources Europe and the Asian part of Turkey
Color The heartwood ranges from straw colored to brown.
Texture Coarse

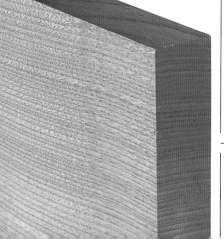

Grain Usually straight but sometimes spiraling
Hardness Hard
Weight Medium, but much lighter than oak (34 lb./cu. ft.) (540 kg/cu. m)
Strength Moderate
Seasoning and stability Liable to checks, splits and honeycombing, and generally slow and difficult to season. But once seasoned it doesn't move much.
Wastage Potentially high with splits, checks or other defects
Range of board widths Good
Range of board thicknesses Should be good, but may depend on yard
Durability Medium, but some insects attack it and the heartwood won't take preservative.

IN THE WORKSHOP

Spanish chestnut has some disadvantages in the workshop; it corrodes ferrous metals and can become stained as a result. Wood with spiraling grain can be difficult to use, but generally it is straight and not interlocking.

Milling Fine; it should not tear excessively and will not dull tools.
Shaping Hard enough to take a good edge or profile.
Assembly Good; glues well.
Finishing Can be polished to a good luster.

VARIATIONS

Though it can be used for decorative veneer, Spanish chestnut is used largely as a secondary lumber, as an alternative to oak. Its most common use is for coffins.

SUSTAINABILITY

There are more common hardwoods in Europe, but as the sweet chestnut is valued for its nuts, its future should not be under threat. There is no real need to buy certified lumber.

AVAILABILITY AND COST

Spanish chestnut is not widely available, but neither is it expensive for a hardwood.

Key uses

Interior
Staircases

Joinery
Internal joinery

Utility
Coppice crafts
Coffins
Casks

Cedrela odorata
West Indian cedar

STRENGTHS
- Aroma
- Interesting grain pattern
- Easy to work
- Stable
- Relatively inexpensive

WEAKNESSES
- Vulnerable to extinction
- Diminishing availability

FAST-GROWING HARDWOOD CEDAR

Though not a true cedar (*Cedrus* species), which would make it a softwood, this species carries the name because of its similarities in look and smell. It is sometimes called cigar-box cedar, as it is used in making humidors. Insects are repelled by the aroma, so the lumber is employed for drawer construction and clothes storage. Otherwise it is very similar to mahogany (*Swietenia macrophylla*) in appearance and texture. It is a fast-growing species, so although it has been overexploited, there is hope for its sustainability.

KEY CHARACTERISTICS
Type Tropical hardwood
Other names Cigar-box cedar, South American cedar, Spanish cedar, species synonym *C. mexicana*
Alternatives Mahogany (*Swietenia macrophylla* or *S. mahogani*)
Sources Central and South America, Florida, West Indies
Color Pink to brown through shades of red, with darker latewood lines
Texture Moderate and even

Grain Generally straight, with distinctive thin, dark red latewood lines
Hardness Soft
Weight Medium (30 lb./cu. ft.) (480 kg/cu. m)
Strength Strong for its weight; used for the construction of racing boats.
Seasoning and stability Seasons easily and fast, and once dry moves moderately.
Wastage Low
Range of board widths Good
Range of board thicknesses Good
Durability Good

IN THE WORKSHOP
West Indian cedar is easy to work in almost every way, and the aromatic smell makes it particularly pleasant to use.

Milling Planes well with little dulling to produce a very smooth finish.
Shaping Takes a good edge or profile, and is easy to cut for making joints.
Assembly Softness means there is some tolerance for a hardwood, but watch out for bruising. Screws, nails and glues well. The lumber does not move much once assembled.
Finishing Can be stained easily and polishes to a good luster.

VARIATIONS
The quartersawn face is rather plain, lacking any rays or patterning.

SUSTAINABILITY
The price of having few weaknesses is that West Indian cedar has been heavily exploited. It is still readily available, but there are real concerns and it has been listed as vulnerable. It regenerates fairly well, and though plantations have been hindered by attack from shoot-boring insects, certified lumber is available.

AVAILABILITY AND COST
Still widely available at moderate prices.

Key uses	Interior Furniture and cabinetmaking	Marine Boat building
	Joinery Interior trim	Utility Cigar boxes

Cedrus libani
Cedar of Lebanon

STRENGTHS
- Aromatic smell
- Repels insects
- Excellent stability
- Available in wide boards

WEAKNESSES
- Knots can be a problem
- Brittle

FRAGRANT SOFTWOOD USED IN DRAWERS
The key characteristics of cedar of Lebanon are its smell and its ability to repel insects, which make it popular for the bottom of drawers and the lining of boxes. The markings are interesting, with gentle color changes from heart to sap and distinct latewood lines, but consistent texture. Cedar trees are often huge, with wide girths, so it is possible to find wide boards in a variety of thicknesses.

KEY CHARACTERISTICS
Type Temperate softwood
Other names True cedar, *C. libanotica*
Alternatives Redwood (*Sequoia sempervirens*), western red cedar (*Thuja plicata*), incense cedar (*Calocedrus decurrens*)
Sources Europe, Middle East
Color Light honey, with a pink-red hue in the latewood lines
Texture Consistent, but a bit furry
Grain Mostly straight, but some gently curving, especially around knots
Hardness Soft to medium

Weight Medium (35 lb./cu. ft.) (560 kg/cu. m)
Strength Poor
Seasoning and stability Easy to season. Very stable with little movement.
Wastage Low
Range of board widths Good, with wide boards available
Range of board thicknesses Varies widely from mill to mill
Durability Poor outside and does not take preservative well; it is not resistant to all pests.

IN THE WORKSHOP
Cedar of Lebanon is frequently used for drawer construction and box linings, but is rarely employed for anything else because other options are cheaper, harder or more decorative. Because wide boards are available there is plenty of quartersawn lumber, which is ideal for drawer bottoms, as it is less likely to move.

Milling Cuts and planes easily and smoothly, but not to a particularly lustrous finish.
Shaping Bruises easily and can chip.
Assembly Glues easily, but watch out for bruising and crushing. Wide boards are often quartersawn, so panels do not need to be glued up from thinner planks.
Finishing Tends to be fairly dull but takes any finish.

SUSTAINABILITY
You are unlikely to find certified cedar of Lebanon, but check for threats in specific countries.

AVAILABILITY AND COST
Reasonably easy to source, but expensive for a softwood and hence used only for specific purposes.

Key uses	Utility	Joinery
	Drawer bottoms	Interior joinery
	Box linings	

Chlorophora excelsa
Iroko

STRENGTHS
- Relatively inexpensive
- Oily and durable
- Hard but lighter than some rivals
- Finishes well

WEAKNESSES
- Interlocking grain
- Bland color and figure
- Only moderately strong

DURABLE HARDWOOD FOR LONG-LASTING JOINERY

Iroko is the utility lumber of the tropical hardwood species. A durable wood, it is used largely for non-decorative purposes, and the oily texture indicates its usefulness for boat building and pilings. Even but coarse, the grain is clearly interlocking and is very difficult to work with hand tools. However, iroko takes a good edge and comes up to a beautiful luster.

KEY CHARACTERISTICS
Type Tropical hardwood
Other names Kambala (Europe)
Similar species *C. regia*
Sources Africa
Color Rich, medium brown with some darker patches
Texture Coarse
Grain Wavy or interlocking
Hardness Hard

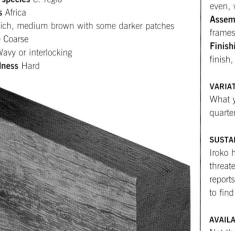

Weight Medium to heavy, but not as heavy as many tropical hardwoods (40 lb./cu. ft.) (640 kg/cu. m)
Strength Moderately strong
Seasoning and stability Easy to season, with little movement once dry
Wastage Low
Range of board widths Good
Range of board thicknesses Good
Durability Good, though sapwood is prone to insect attack

IN THE WORKSHOP
The downside of finding a species that is easy to season, has few defects and is a durable wood for doors and windows is that its interlocking grain makes manufacture awkward.

Milling Not only is the grain often interlocking, but it can carry abrasive deposits that dull blades and cutters. Keep passes shallow, especially when planing quartersawn sides.
Shaping Iroko is popular for joinery because the texture is even, which makes joint-cutting relatively simple.
Assembly With little movement, iroko is good for making frames, and it glues well.
Finishing The coarse grain may need filling for a fine finish, but the surface is hard and takes polish well.

VARIATIONS
What you see is what you get with iroko, and quartersawn and plain-sawn sides differ very little.

SUSTAINABILITY
Iroko has been designated as vulnerable on some lists of threatened species, though other, more authoritative reports say it is at a low risk only. It is not an easy lumber to find from a certified source, though that may improve.

AVAILABILITY AND COST
Not the most expensive tropical hardwood, and available from yards that stock exotics.

Key uses	Joinery	Marine
	External joinery Frames	Boat building

Cordia dodecandra
Ziricote

STRENGTHS
- Exquisite appearance
- Hard and heavy
- Easy to work

WEAKNESSES
- Rare and expensive
- Prone to surface checking

DISTINCTIVE GRAIN THAT RESEMBLES WALNUT

Though it combines the appearance and texture of the best walnut with that of the best rosewood, ziricote is not widely used, possibly because it is expensive and in limited supply. It has a rich dark brown color, with irregular thin, wavy black lines. It can be a large, dominant tree but it is not found in one particular area, and is often stunted, hence the restricted supply.

KEY CHARACTERISTICS
Type Tropical hardwood
Other names Sericote, ziracote
Alternatives European oak (*Quercus robur*)
Sources Southern Mexico, Belize, Guatemala
Color Rich dark brown with thin black lines. Some silvery flecking where rays are randomly revealed.
Texture Fine to medium and even
Grain Straightish, with slight wave
Hardness Very hard
Weight Heavy (c. 55 lb./cu. ft.) (880 kg/cu. m)
Strength Strong
Seasoning and stability Difficult to season, with risk of surface checking, but very stable once dry.

Wastage Should be relatively low, especially when contrasting white sapwood is integrated into a project.
Range of board widths Wide boards should be available, as the tree grows up to 30 inches in diameter.
Range of board thicknesses May be limited by restricted supply.
Durability Moderate

IN THE WORKSHOP

For such a hard wood, ziricote is surprisingly easy to work, better than many rosewoods and other tropical hardwoods. It turns and carves well, though the grain patterns are probably best displayed on flat surfaces.

Milling Surfaces well, with little risk of chipping or tearing.
Shaping Takes a superb edge or profile, and does not dull edges too quickly.
Assembly Glues fairly well, though test first, as it is on the oily side. You will need to drill pilot holes for screws and nails. Very stable once dry.
Finishing Polishes to a superb luster and does not need staining.

VARIATIONS

Best quartersawn to reveal the black wavy lines. Buy quartersawn veneer if it is available.

SUSTAINABILITY

It is very difficult to establish the status of a lumber like ziricote, as it grows randomly and is not exploited in the quantities of, say, West Indian cedar. There is an argument that buying rare species like ziricote benefits local economies and puts a value on trees that might otherwise be felled for land. You are unlikely to find certified ziricote.

AVAILABILITY AND COST

Only available from specialist importers, and very expensive.

Key uses	Interior	Luxury & leisure
	Quality furniture	Gunstocks
	Cabinetmaking	
	Flooring	Decorative
		Turning
	Joinery	Carving
	Paneling	Veneer

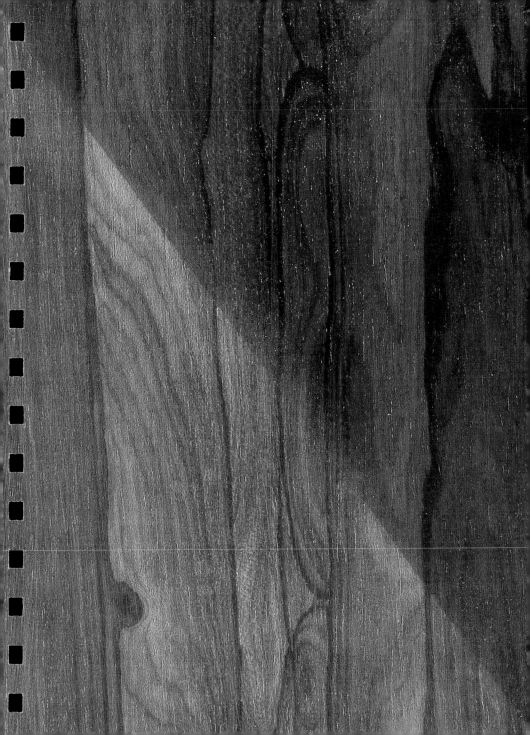

Cordia elaeagnoides
Bocote

STRENGTHS
- Distinctive grain
- Relatively easy to work

WEAKNESSES
- Few wide boards available
- High wastage

HARDWOOD WITH DRAMATIC STRIPES

Bocote has dramatic patterning and is hard, heavy and surprisingly easy to work considering the distinctive grain. It is stable, though difficult to season, so there may be an issue with wastage due to checking or splits. As the roundwood is often narrow, the boards may have a high proportion of pale sapwood, which adds to wastage problems.

KEY CHARACTERISTICS
Type Tropical hardwood
Other names Canatele
Sources Central America, West Indies
Color Light golden brown with regular dark brown lines
Texture Fine to medium, and uniform
Grain Straight
Hardness Hard
Weight Heavy (50 lb./cu. ft.) (800 kg/cu. m)

AVAILABILITY AND SUSTAINABILITY
A fair number of suppliers stock bocote. It is not listed as vulnerable by authoritative reports but there are concerns regarding its sustainability. It is likely to be expensive.

Key uses **Interior** Furniture Flooring   **Decorative** Veneer

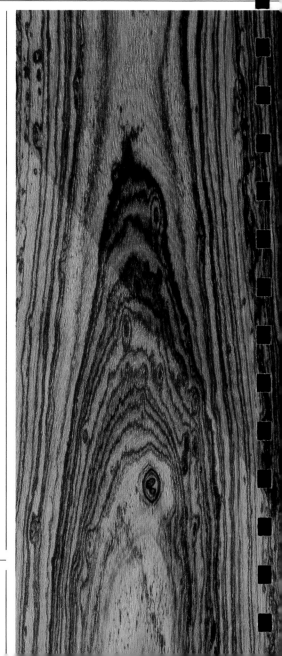

Cybistax donnell-smithii
Primavera

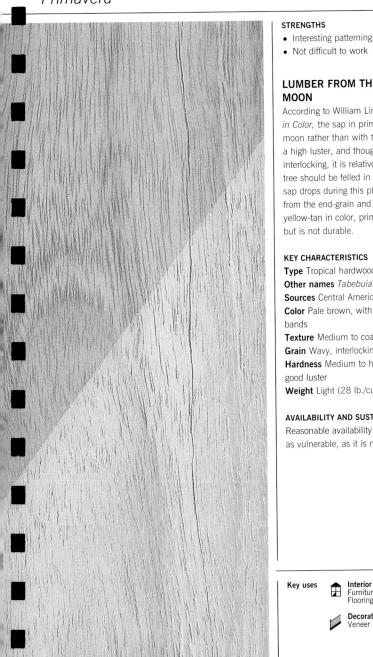

STRENGTHS
- Interesting patterning
- Not difficult to work

WEAKNESSES
- Tends to split
- Interlocking grain

LUMBER FROM THE DARK SIDE OF THE MOON

According to William Lincoln, author of *World Woods in Color,* the sap in primavera rises and falls with the moon rather than with the seasons, as is normal. It has a high luster, and though the grain can be irregular and interlocking, it is relatively easy to work. However, the tree should be felled in the "dark of the moon," as the sap drops during this phase, and less will then seep from the end-grain and attract insects. A medium yellow-tan in color, primavera has intriguing patterning but is not durable.

KEY CHARACTERISTICS
Type Tropical hardwood
Other names *Tabebuia donnell-smithii*, roble
Sources Central America
Color Pale brown, with darker lines and some yellow bands
Texture Medium to coarse
Grain Wavy, interlocking or straight
Hardness Medium to hard; moderately strong with a good luster
Weight Light (28 lb./cu. ft.) (450 kg/cu. m)

AVAILABILITY AND SUSTAINABILITY
Reasonable availability and cost. Primavera is not listed as vulnerable, as it is not a prime commercial species.

Key uses

Interior
Furniture
Flooring

Decorative
Veneer

Joinery
Interior trim
General joinery
Paneling

Dalbergia cearensis
Kingwood

STRENGTHS
- Spectacular grain pattern
- Intriguing pinky brown color with contrasting sapwood
- Straight grain

WEAKNESSES
- Risk of knots
- Prone to checking and splits
- Rare and expensive

SMALLER ROSEWOOD WITH DISTINCTIVE PATTERN

Kingwood is one of the rosewoods, with fantastic grain patterning and color, but it suffers from being only a relatively small tree. As a result there is a risk of heart shakes on any board, and the dramatically contrasting pale sapwood, if not integrated into a design, can be very wasteful. The trunk is rarely wider than 10 inches in diameter.

KEY CHARACTERISTICS
Type Tropical hardwood
Other names Violetwood, violete, violet kingwood
Sources Brazil
Color Pink or light red to rich dark brown, with yellow-cream sapwood
Texture Fine and even
Grain Straight, but there can be inconsistency in the density of the growth rings.
Hardness Hard

Weight Very heavy (75 lb./cu. ft.) (1200 kg/cu. m)
Strength Strong, but considered brittle
Seasoning and stability Prone to checking while it seasons. Stable once dry.
Wastage Trees with a small diameter tend to have high wastage, with a high proportion of sapwood and the risk of heart shakes.
Range of board widths Very limited, with boards no wider than about 8 inches, and usually narrower.
Range of board thicknesses Limited
Durability Thought to be durable

IN THE WORKSHOP
The challenge of working with kingwood is overcoming the inherent problems of small-diameter lumber, but more often than not it is available only as veneer.

Milling Good, but tools must be very sharp.
Shaping Will make a superb profile or molding.
Assembly Check first before gluing, as the surface can be waxy. Pilot holes are needed for screws and nails.
Finishing Finishes to a superb luster.

VARIATIONS
Any veneer or board is likely to incorporate both plain-sawn and quartersawn sections. Consider using the contrasting sapwood for effect.

SUSTAINABILITY
Though it has not been listed as endangered, kingwood is always likely to be in short supply, and you are unlikely to find certified lumber.

AVAILABILITY AND COST
Very rare and very expensive.

Key uses — Decorative: Veneer, Marquetry, Decorative inlay, Turning

Utility: Small fittings

Dalbergia latifolia
Indian rosewood

STRENGTHS
- Color and pattern
- Strength and density

WEAKNESSES
- Difficult to use
- Limited availability
- Doubtful sustainability
- Expensive

GOOD QUALITY PLANTATION LUMBER

It is not easy to describe Indian rosewood, as one piece is so different from the next, as is true of so many of the *Dalbergia* species. Generally a very dark brown, with a medium-coarse texture, the lumber features intrusive purple-red, pink and cream streaks. The grain is closely interlocking but otherwise straight or gently curving. Confirming the source of Indian rosewood is unlikely to be easy, and there are concerns regarding illegal logging, though plantation-grown lumber, known as sonekeling, is probably safer. Durable and hard, Indian rosewood is popular for both furniture making and ornamental turning. It is also used as a veneer for interiors, doors and cabinets.

KEY CHARACTERISTICS
Type Tropical hardwood
Other names Sonekeling, East Indian rosewood
Similar species *D. javanica*, *D. sissoo*
Alternatives Other rosewoods (*Dalbergia* species),
European walnut (*Juglans regia*)
Sources India

Color Dark brown, with wild streaks of cream, purple-red and pink
Texture Medium to coarse
Grain Straight or gently curving, but also interlocking
Hardness Very hard
Weight Heavy (52 lb./cu. ft.) (830 kg/cu. m)
Strength Generally strong
Seasoning and stability Color improves during seasoning, which should ideally be slow and in a kiln to minimize degradation. Very stable.
Wastage Only problem is likely to arise from limited range of boards to suit specific needs.
Range of board widths Limited
Range of board thicknesses Limited
Durability Very durable

IN THE WORKSHOP

Unfortunately, Indian rosewood contains abrasive deposits that exaggerate its tendency to dull tool edges.

Milling Very hard to cut and surface.
Shaping Takes a superb edge and profile, but is tough on cutters.
Assembly Will not accept nails, though most woodworkers would be unlikely to use them for the sort of work that rosewood is suited to. Glues and screws well.
Finishing Coarse grain needs filling, but otherwise fine as it does not have the oiliness of other rosewoods.

VARIATIONS

Quartersawn lumber has a ribbon figure.

SUSTAINABILITY

Reportedly vulnerable and overexploited. Apparently, true Indian rosewood is protected by the Indian Forest Act and cannot be exported in log or board form. However, sonekeling, the plantation lumber, is certainly available.

AVAILABILITY AND COST

Not widely available, and likely to be expensive.

Key uses			
Interior Furniture Cabinetmaking		**Joinery** Quality interior joinery	
Decorative Veneer for interiors, doors and cabinetmaking		**Luxury & leisure** Musical instruments	
		Marine Boat building	

Dalbergia nigra
Brazilian rosewood

STRENGTHS
- Superb figure
- Good color range
- Hard and strong

WEAKNESSES
- Very expensive
- Uncertain sustainability
- Limited supply

ONE OF THE WORLD'S MOST PRIZED LUMBERS

Hard and heavy, Brazilian rosewood has some of the coloring and patterning of English walnut (*Juglans regia*). The range of colors, from light honey to very dark brown, makes it extremely attractive, while its weight, strength and ability to take a sharp edge mean it is ideal for furniture and cabinetmaking. The texture is even and fine to medium, with relatively straight grain and not much interlocking. It is not surprising that Brazilian rosewood is so expensive, and that the species is all but extinct and subject to trade restrictions.

KEY CHARACTERISTICS
Type Tropical hardwood
Other names Santos rosewood, jacaranda
Alternatives Other rosewoods (*Dalbergia* species), jacaranda do para (*D. spruceana*), jacaranda pardo (*Machaerium villosum*)
Sources Brazil
Color Light to very dark brown, with a reddish hue
Texture Fine to medium, and even
Grain Slightly wavy
Hardness Very hard

Weight Heavy (53 lb./cu. ft.) (850 kg/cu. m)
Strength Strong and relatively easy to bend
Seasoning and stability Season slow and ideally in a kiln to reduce degradation. Very stable once dry.
Wastage Should be low
Range of board widths Limited
Range of board thicknesses Limited
Durability Very good

IN THE WORKSHOP

Though its grain is relatively straight, Brazilian rosewood is not the easiest of lumbers to work. Like many related species it is oily, which affects edges, glues and finishes.

Milling Dulls tools quickly, but surfaces nicely.
Shaping Takes a superb edge.
Assembly Gluing can be difficult, so experiment with small offcuts first. You may need to apply adhesive to both faces.
Finishing Needs care, as its oiliness interferes with the finish. Experiment on offcuts.

VARIATIONS

Brazilian rosewood is consistently decorative, and because of its value it is often sliced for veneer.

SUSTAINABILITY

Brazilian rosewood has been listed on the CITES Appendix I, which means the species is threatened with extinction and that trade should be limited and controlled. Its inclusion on Appendix I gives it some protection, by making the exporting country responsible for the integrity of the harvest. Make sure you know which rosewood you are buying, as it can be difficult to distinguish between them; then research its current status to decide whether or not to buy.

AVAILABILITY AND COST

Very expensive and available only in limited quantities.

Key uses

Interior	Furniture making
	Flooring
Luxury & leisure	Musical instruments
Decorative	Veneer for cabinetmaking
	Turning

Dalbergia retusa
Cocobolo

STRENGTHS
- Contrasting range of colors
- Distinctive grain pattern
- Hard and dense

WEAKNESSES
- Very limited supply
- Expensive
- Poor seasoning

DECORATIVE ROSEWOOD IN SHORT SUPPLY

Like many of its rosewood cousins, cocobolo is highly prized for its distinctive grain pattern and color, for its marvelous luster and for its hardness and density. As it takes a sharp edge or profile, it is commonly used for detail work by ornamental turners and furniture makers. Cocobolo has many of the qualities of, say, ebony, but more color and pattern. These will, however, diminish with age, as with so many of the *Dalbergia* species.

KEY CHARACTERISTICS
Type Tropical hardwood
Other names Nicaragua rosewood, granadillo
Similar species Tulipwood (*D. decipularis*), Brazilwood (*Caesalpinia echinata*)
Alternatives Snakewood (*Brosimum aubletti*)
Sources Central America
Color Streaks of red, orange and yellow amid darker bands; with age the lighter streaks darken to a rich red.
Texture Fine and even
Grain Irregular
Hardness Very hard

Weight Very heavy (65 lb./cu. ft.) (1040 kg/cu. m)
Strength Very strong
Seasoning and stability Slow to season, with a high risk of distortion and checking, but very stable once dry.
Wastage Should be low, but boards may be available only in limited dimensions.
Range of board widths Likely to be limited
Range of board thicknesses Likely to be limited
Durability Very oily, so naturally durable, but this is not a lumber you are likely to use for fence posts! It is popular for cutlery handles, as it is waterproof.

IN THE WORKSHOP
Working with this hard lumber is a challenge for any woodworker, because it can be a dusty experience. The dust from such exotics as cocobolo can cause breathing and skin problems.

Milling Blades need to be sharp, but an extremely smooth surface is relatively easy to achieve.
Shaping Hard lumber like cocobolo takes the finest of edges, and is ideal for profiling or for ornamental turning.
Assembly Like other "rosewoods," cocobolo is oily by nature, so a few experiments are recommended for gluing. Holes for screws and nails need to be pre-drilled.
Finishing Finishes well and accepts stain, though few woodworkers would ever consider such an option.

VARIATIONS
Highly figured logs are often made into veneer for inlay and decoration.

SUSTAINABILITY
There is very little certified cocobolo, and the species has been reported as vulnerable. It is well worth asking suppliers about their sources or considering an alternative.

AVAILABILITY AND COST
Limited supply and very expensive.

Key uses | **Decorative** Ornamental turning Inlay and features in furniture Veneer for paneling | **Utility** Cutlery handles
Luxury & leisure Musical instruments

Dalbergia stevensonii
Honduras rosewood

STRENGTHS
- Dense and heavy
- Resonant
- Beautiful figure
- Fine texture

WEAKNESSES
- High wastage
- Oily patches can reject glue
- Expensive

TOUGHEST AND MOST MUSICAL ROSEWOOD

Honduras rosewood has a distinctive look and feel, not dissimilar to beli (*Paraberlinia bifoliolata*), but it is much darker. It has some of the subtle coloring of the walnuts, particularly English walnut. The texture is fine to medium but the grain is often interlocking and difficult to work, especially by hand. The beautiful wavy grain and exquisite coloring (from medium brown to black with purple flecks) make it ideal as a veneer, and its high price often limits it to this use. Being dense and resonant, it is also used for making xylophone and marimba bars.

KEY CHARACTERISTICS

Type Tropical hardwood
Other names Nogaed (U.S.)
Alternatives Other rosewoods (*Dalbergia* species), European walnut (*Juglans regia*)
Sources Belize
Color Medium brown to black, with some purple and red flecks
Texture Fine to medium

Grain Usually wavy or interlocking, with irregular bands; occasionally straight
Hardness Hard
Weight Heavy (59 lb./cu. ft.) (940 kg/cu. m)
Strength Tough and dense
Seasoning and stability Needs slow seasoning to avoid degradation but moves very little once dry.
Wastage Can be very high if you are looking for straight-grained lengths.
Range of board widths Likely to be limited
Range of board thicknesses Likely to be limited
Durability Very good

IN THE WORKSHOP

You have to be looking for a special effect, or a special sound, to bring Honduras rosewood into your workshop.

Milling Warning: this lumber will dull your tools. That said, a good surface can be achieved, especially on straight-grained lengths.
Shaping Ornamental turners enjoy working with Honduras rosewood, and it can be worked to the sharpest of edges. The texture is relatively fine, so it can be machined to an exact profile.
Assembly Watch out for oily patches that may reject glue and make assembly awkward. Fortunately, the wood does not move much afterward.
Finishing Will not take a natural finish like wax, and care is needed when applying a varnish or polish.

VARIATIONS

Few. Select carefully and you will find the patterning you need, but expect some wastage in the process.

SUSTAINABILITY

Surprisingly for a rosewood, this species is rarely listed as threatened, but there isn't much certified supply.

AVAILABILITY AND COST

Honduras rosewood is expensive, is available only rarely, and only from specialist suppliers.

Key uses

Luxury & leisure
Musical instruments

Interior
Furniture

Decorative
Veneer for cabinetmaking and interior paneling

Diospyros celebica
Macassar ebony

STRENGTHS
- Distinctive grain pattern
- Very hard and heavy
- Very stable once dry

WEAKNESSES
- Dust can irritate
- Slow and difficult to season
- Risk of checks and splits

EXOTIC, EXPENSIVE DECORATIVE HARDWOOD

Grown on the Indonesian island of Sulawesi (formerly known as Celebes), this is one of the rarest and most expensive woods you can buy. It is distinguished by the stripy grain pattern, which is largely dark brown or black but interspersed with much paler bands. The scarcity of the lumber is not helped by the tree's relatively small size.

KEY CHARACTERISTICS

Type Tropical hardwood
Other names *D. ebenum*, *D. macassar*, Indian ebony, coromandel (U.K.), Sri Lankan ebony
Similar species African ebony (*D. crassiflora*), Indian ebony (*D. tomentosa* and *D. melanoxylon*), Andaman ebony (*D. marmorata*)
Sources Sulawesi, Indonesia
Color Stripes of dark brown and black, with lighter yellow or beige bands
Texture Fine to medium and even
Grain Generally straight, but there may be some interlocking or wavy grain.

Hardness Very dense and hard
Weight Very heavy (68 lb./cu. ft.) (1090 kg/cu. m)
Strength Generally used for decoration, not because the heart can be brittle but because it is so expensive.
Seasoning and stability Very slow to season; the tree is often ringbarked (girdled) for two years before felling to start the drying process. Liable to split if dried too quickly. Very stable once seasoned.
Wastage Low
Range of board widths May well be limited
Range of board thicknesses May well be limited
Durability Very durable against rot, but some risk of insect attack

IN THE WORKSHOP

Because of its cost and scarcity, this is not a lumber to experiment with. It is very hard, but is not considered to dull edges too badly. The dust is reported to irritate some people's skin.

Milling You may need to reduce the angle on the edge of blades, and there is a risk of tearing when surfacing.
Shaping Takes a good edge for profiling.
Assembly Screws and nails will need pre-drilling, but the lumber glues well.
Finishing Finishes to an incredibly smooth, high luster.

VARIATIONS

Macassar ebony is often cut for veneer, but there is not much difference between plain-sawn and quartersawn faces.

SUSTAINABILITY

Supposedly felled only by quota, but it has been listed as vulnerable. Certified lumber is unlikely to be available. There are few alternatives.

AVAILABILITY AND COST

Not widely available, and very expensive.

Key uses   **Interior** Cabinetmaking   **Luxury & leisure** Musical instruments

Decorative Ornamental turning Inlay

Diospyros crassiflora
African ebony

STRENGTHS
- Amazing color
- Hard, heavy and dense

WEAKNESSES
- Liable to splits, checks and defects
- Very expensive and rare
- Few certified supplies
- Variable color

THE BLACKEST OF ALL WOOD
Ebonies can be difficult to identify, as they are all heavy and black and there is some confusion regarding their names. African ebony is sometimes mixed up with Gabon ebony (*D. dendo*) on suppliers' inventories. The color is much the same, though African ebony is reportedly the blackest of all, with just a few paler gray or beige streaks.

KEY CHARACTERISTICS
Type Tropical hardwood
Other names Sometimes named after country of origin (Nigerian ebony, Cameroon ebony, etc.)
Similar species *D. piscatoria*, Gabon ebony (*D. dendo*)
Alternatives Macassar ebony (*D. celebica*), English oak (*Quercus robur*)
Sources Central and West Africa
Color Mostly black, but some black or gray streaks. Very dark when finished.
Texture Very fine and even
Grain Straight, with some interlocking
Hardness Very hard

Weight Very heavy (63 lb./cu. ft.) (1000 kg/cu. m)
Strength Very strong and resistant to shocks and heavy loads. Surprisingly good for bending, though it is unlikely to be used for that.
Seasoning and stability Quick to season and stable once dry
Wastage Supply is so limited that you may encounter boards with splits or streaks that are hard to avoid, but the lumber is likely to be used for smaller components, so wastage can be managed moderately well.
Range of board widths Limited
Range of board thicknesses Limited
Durability Very durable, though some risk of insect attack to *D. piscatoria*.

IN THE WORKSHOP
Any ebony is tough on tools and very hard to work, and some woodworkers find the dust is irritating to the skin, eyes and lungs.

Milling Because it is so hard, there is great risk of boards chattering as you plane, so keep cuts to a minimum. There is much to be said for using some kind of sanding machine or device for planing hard woods like ebony.
Shaping Ideal for intricate turning or carving and takes a superb edge, but low-angle cutters may need to be used.
Assembly Glues well enough, though the surface is so dense it is almost metallic, so experiment first. Pilot drilling for screws and nails will be essential.
Finishing Experiment first with polishes, as oils can sit on the dense surface. Make sure any excess is wiped away. Produces an excellent luster.

VARIATIONS
Often converted into veneer.

SUSTAINABILITY
D. crassiflora has been listed as endangered by IUCN. There is no evidence of certified supplies.

AVAILABILITY AND COST
It is very expensive and increasingly rare.

Key uses			
	Decorative Ornamental turning Inlay		**Luxury & leisure** Musical instruments
	Technical Measuring instruments		**Utility** Cutlery Small fittings and handles

Dyera costulata
Jelutong

STRENGTHS
- Fine and even texture
- Creamy yellow color
- Easy to carve

WEAKNESSES
- No figure
- Lacks strength and durability
- Latex gum pockets

FINE AND EVEN HARDWOOD FOR CARVERS

Lightweight and with little discernible grain pattern, jelutong has a fine, even texture that makes it ideal for patternmaking and carving, while lacking the figure needed for more decorative work. Otherwise it is largely considered a utility species, with the only feature being occasional small pockets of latex (used in chewing gum), which appear as tiny fissures and cannot always be avoided, although some woodworkers use them as a visual effect. It resembles common boxwood (*Buxus sempervirens*) in color, but in no other respect.

KEY CHARACTERISTICS
Type Tropical hardwood
Alternatives Common boxwood (*Buxus sempervirens*), European linden (*Tilia x europaea*), basswood (*T. americana*)
Sources Southeast Asia
Color Pale yellow, turning to cream or straw
Texture Fine and even
Grain Fairly straight
Hardness Medium-soft for a tropical hardwood

Weight Light (28 lb./cu. ft.) (450 kg/cu. m)
Strength Weak
Seasoning and stability Quick and simple to season, and there is very little movement after drying.
Wastage Staining from seasoning and latex pockets may be hard to avoid and can increase wastage rates, though jelutong is rarely used for its looks.
Range of board widths Reasonable
Range of board thicknesses Usually thicker boards aimed at carvers and patternmakers
Durability Poor

IN THE WORKSHOP

You will not find jelutong in many workshops, but for the carver or patternmaker it is a valuable alternative to basswood (*Tilia americana*) or white pine (*Pinus strobus*). Its great assets are the fine, even texture and creamy color.

Milling Most carvers do not plane jelutong much, but it can be worked easily enough, without much tearing and without dulling tools.
Shaping One of the reasons why jelutong is popular with carvers and patternmakers is that it can be carved into an exact shape with sharp edges.
Assembly Jelutong glues well, so laminating blocks for carving poses few problems.
Finishing Produces a nice luster, though the figure is bland and few woodworkers use it without paint or stain.

VARIATIONS
The latex pockets can be used for effect.

SUSTAINABILITY
As a rule, softer, lighter lumber normally comes from faster-growing trees that are not being harvested to death. That is certainly true of jelutong, which does not appear on lists of endangered species.

AVAILABILITY AND COST
Available from specialist suppliers, but not expensive.

Key uses **Decorative** Carving Patternmaking   **Joinery** Plywood

Entandrophragma cylindricum
Sapele

STRENGTHS
- Inexpensive
- Consistent
- Possible alternative to mahogany

WEAKNESSES
- Bland
- Moderate stability
- Interlocking grain

INFERIOR RELATIVE OF MAHOGANY

Sapele might be considered as a utility substitute for mahogany, and indeed it belongs to the same Meliaceae family. It has a similar color and a fairly straight grain, but rather unattractive dark bands. However, the species is favored when the figuring is good. Not surprisingly, it is used largely as a veneer for the manufacture of office furniture or store interiors, and in the solid for joinery, particularly doors. Though the texture is relatively fine and even, the grain can be interlocking and awkward to work.

KEY CHARACTERISTICS
Type Tropical hardwood
Alternatives Mahogany (*Swietenia* species), jarrah (*Eucalyptus marginata*), Red River gum (*Eucalyptus camaldulensis*)
Sources Africa
Color Medium red-brown, with richer, darker bands
Texture Fine to medium
Grain Fairly straight, though some wood is wavy and interlocking
Hardness Soft for a hardwood

Weight Medium (39 lb./cu. ft.) (620 kg/cu. m)
Strength Not strong, with a tendency to buckle
Seasoning and stability Prone to distortion during seasoning, especially if rapid, and to some movement once dry.
Wastage Low
Range of board widths Good
Range of board thicknesses Good
Durability Medium

IN THE WORKSHOP
Sapele is not the easiest lumber to work with, as it is dusty and has an interlocking grain, but it finishes well.

Milling Interlocking grain leads to frequent tears when machining. This is one of the few lumbers that is easier to work by hand.
Shaping Takes a good edge or profile.
Assembly Glues well, and movement is limited.
Finishing Stains well, with care, and finishes cleanly.

VARIATIONS
There is some ribbon figuring on quartersawn cuts, with some fiddleback or even mottling, both of which are used for veneers.

SUSTAINABILITY
The status varies from one country to another, and deserves research, but there is little evidence of certified supplies.

AVAILABILITY AND COST
Mainly available as plywood, but can be bought in the solid from specialist importers of exotics. Prices are mid-range.

Key uses

Interior
Furniture and cabinetmaking
Flooring

Joinery
Interior trim
Paneling
Plywood

Eucalyptus marginata
Jarrah

STRENGTHS
- Rich color
- Beautiful figure
- Tough, hard and lustrous

WEAKNESSES
- Inconsistent color
- Interlocking grain
- Hard to work

RED GUM ONCE USED FOR RAILROAD TIES
Jarrah is strong and naturally durable, so much so that it used to be employed in railroad building for ties. It grows only in a narrow strip along the west coast of Australia south of Perth, and is used locally for anything from house building to the making of fine furniture.

KEY CHARACTERISTICS
Type Temperate hardwood
Other names Western Australian mahogany
Alternatives Purpleheart (*Peltogyne paniculata*)
Sources Western Australia
Color Rich red or reddish brown, varying from medium to dark; any red tends to darken to brown with age. Can be flecked with small stains for a mottled effect.
Texture Moderate to coarse
Grain Straight, but with some wave, and can be interlocking.
Hardness Hard
Weight Heavy, but varies (50 lb./cu. ft.) (800 kg/cu. m)
Strength Strong, but not ideal for bending unless grain is straight.
Seasoning and stability Best air-dried initially, as jarrah can warp in the kiln.

Wastage Moderate, mainly because you have to watch out for occasional gum pockets, which can be used as a feature.
Range of board widths Good
Range of board thicknesses Good where stock is readily available
Durability Good

IN THE WORKSHOP
Jarrah is used for all sorts of building tasks in Western Australia, and is one of the preferred species for furniture makers and woodturners in the region. It is certainly hard, and blades will need regular sharpening for a good finish.

Milling Fine to plane, but edges must be very sharp to cope with the hardness. Working by hand is difficult.
Shaping Takes a good edge and looks good with fine profiles or more rounded features.
Assembly Nails and screws may need pre-drilling, but the lumber will not split.
Finishing Produces a lovely luster and has an interesting color range. Can be finished with any polish, and takes stain well.

VARIATIONS
Jarrah burl is very popular for turning and carving, as it has good color and a texture that suggests a degree of softness, even though the wood is actually hard. Quartersawn cuts sometimes reveal mottled rays.

SUSTAINABILITY
Not listed as vulnerable, but there is little evidence of certified jarrah supplies.

AVAILABILITY AND COST
Jarrah isn't common in North America, but when it can be found the stocks should be good and the price somewhere between expensive and moderate.

Key uses   **Interior** Furniture making Flooring   ↗ **Construction** House building

Decorative Turning   **Exterior** Railroad ties

Euxylophora paraensis
Pau amarello

STRENGTHS
- Heavy, hard and tough
- Creamy texture
- Bright yellow color

WEAKNESSES
- Grain can be interlocking
- Little figure
- May be difficult to find

YELLOW BOXWOOD FROM BRAZIL

Pau amarello combines the bright yellow color and grain pattern of jelutong (*Dyera costulata*) with the hardness of common boxwood (*Buxus sempervirens*). Indeed, the Smithsonian Institution lists it as one of the many woods that are known as boxwood, most of which are hard, heavy and tough, and are commonly used for mallets, tool handles, printers' blocks and rulers. Typically pau amarello has a fine texture, with darker and lighter patches shimmering across the pattern and hinting at an interlocking grain. The end-grain has distinct lines of earlywood and latewood, which do not show up on the face.

KEY CHARACTERISTICS
Type Tropical hardwood
Other names Yellowheart
Alternatives Common boxwood (*Buxus sempervirens*), bastard box (*Eucalyptus cypellocarpa*), American holly (*Ilex opaca*)
Sources Lower reaches of the Amazon in Brazil
Color Yellow
Texture Fine to medium; even
Grain Curving and interlocking

Hardness Hard
Weight Heavy (c. 54 lb./cu. ft.) (860 kg/cu. m)
Strength Good
Seasoning and stability Shrinks evenly during seasoning, and without much distortion. Not thought to move much in use.
Wastage Sapwood is almost indistinguishable from the heartwood, and with few defects and little distortion there should be low wastage.
Range of board widths Probably limited
Range of board thicknesses Likely to be limited
Durability Good

IN THE WORKSHOP

The wavy, interlocking grain of pau amarello has short fibers that chip easily, though woodworkers do not consider this species to be difficult to work.

Milling You may have problems where the grain is interlocking, but otherwise milling is easy. The wood should not dull tools, as the texture is smooth.
Shaping Takes a beautiful edge, being hard and dense.
Assembly Glues, screws and nails well.
Finishing Not oily, and finishes well with fine sanding. Has a good luster.

VARIATIONS

Figured pau amarello, with curly patterning in the grain, is known as pau setim. This can be very difficult to plane, and is best sanded for surfacing because of likely tearing.

SUSTAINABILITY

Pau amarello is the sort of lesser-known species from tropical rain forests that is sometimes available from certified sources, but it will not be common. It has not been listed as vulnerable, and its use should probably be encouraged.

AVAILABILITY AND COST

Pau amarello is available from some specialist dealers. It is usually cheaper than common boxwood.

Key uses **Interior**
Furniture
Flooring

 Utility
Tool handles

Fagus grandifolia
American beech

STRENGTHS

- Consistent grain and texture
- Easy to use
- Inexpensive
- Hard and strong

WEAKNESSES

- High degree of movement
- Uninteresting figure
- Yellows with age

UTILITY TIMBER ONCE POPULAR FOR CHAIRS

Beech is used extensively in mass-produced furniture because it is easy to work, consistent and inexpensive. It is not, however, especially decorative, so is often finished with paint or stain, both of which it takes very well. Medullary rays, which appear as tiny dark flecks in quarter-cut and slab-cut boards, are a distinguishing feature.

KEY CHARACTERISTICS

Type Temperate hardwood
Alternatives Yellow birch (*Betula alleghaniensis*), poplar (*Populus* species)
Sources North America
Color Reddish brown
Texture Even and generally fine, but coarser than European beech
Grain Straight and defect-free
Hardness Hard
Weight Medium to heavy (46 lb./cu. ft.) (740 kg/cu. m)

Strength Very strong, and good for steam bending
Seasoning and stability Tends to move more than most temperate hardwoods, both from green and in the workshop, and it needs to be seasoned well. Tends not to be used for wide panels, except as a veneer. Make sure it is dry before use.
Wastage Low, as there is little sapwood and few defects.
Range of board widths Good
Range of board thicknesses Good, with thick stock available
Durability Needs preservatives for external use. Prone to insect attack and not durable to decay, but can be preserved.

IN THE WORKSHOP

Woodworkers tend to favor it for structural purposes, workshop jigs and doweling, as the figure and color are uninteresting, or for work that is to be painted or stained. It is often used to make reproduction furniture because its indistinct grain can be disguised as other woods.

Milling Very simple. Grain is straight and easy to work, though it can bind on saw blades and burn.
Shaping Takes an edge really well. Good for turning, and is used for many turned components.
Assembly Glues easily and is neither too hard nor too soft for clamping. Nails do not require pre-drilling.
Finishing Takes any finish evenly, and is often painted or stained. With a clear finish it yellows unpleasantly within a few years.

VARIATIONS

Steamed beech tends to be darker and redder.

SUSTAINABILITY

Certified supplies are available, though there is no great threat to beech.

AVAILABILITY AND COST

Easy to buy, and one of the cheapest temperate hardwoods, at nearly half the cost of oak or cherry.

Key uses **Interior** Bentwood furniture Mass-produced furniture

 Technical Workshop jigs

Joinery Doweling and compressed biscuits Store interiors

Fagus sylvatica
European beech

STRENGTHS	WEAKNESSES
• Consistent grain and texture	• High level of movement
• Easy to use	• Uninteresting figure
• Inexpensive	• Yellows with age
• Hard and strong	

UTILITY LUMBER ONCE POPULAR FOR CHAIRMAKING

Beech won its spurs, so to speak, in the Chiltern woodlands of southeast England, where turners known as bodgers turned chair legs and stretchers from the pale pink hardwood. Beech is still used extensively in mass-produced furniture because it is very easy to work, consistent and inexpensive. It is often painted or stained, taking finishes very well. Medullary rays, which appear as tiny dark flecks in quarter-cut and slab-cut boards, are a distinguishing feature.

KEY CHARACTERISTICS
Type Temperate hardwood
Other names English beech
Alternatives Yellow birch (*Betula alleghaniensis*), London plane (*Platanus acerifolia*), poplar (*Populus* species), Japanese oak (*Quercus mongolica*)
Sources Europe
Color Light brown with a pinkish hue
Texture Consistent and close-grained; very smooth when sanded

Grain Straight and free of defects
Hardness Hard
Weight Medium to heavy (45 lb./cu. ft.) (720 kg/cu. m)
Strength Very strong; good for steam bending
Seasoning and stability Tends to move more than most temperate hardwoods, both from the green and in the workshop, and it needs to be seasoned well. Seasoning is fast. Tends not to be used for wide panels.
Wastage Low
Range of board widths Good
Range of board thicknesses Good, with thick stock available
Durability Needs preservative for external use

IN THE WORKSHOP

Because of its strength and consistency, European beech is popular for steam bending, especially in mass production. It is often used to produce reproduction furniture because its indistinct grain can be disguised as other woods.

Milling Very simple; grain is straight and easy to work.
Shaping Takes an edge very well.
Assembly Glues easily and is neither too hard nor too soft for clamping.
Finishing Takes any finish evenly, and is often painted or stained. With a clear finish it yellows unpleasantly within a few years.

VARIATIONS

Steamed beech tends to be darker and redder. European beech is also famous for spalting, with darker diseased lines or veins running through the wood.

SUSTAINABILITY

European beech is under attack from gray squirrels, which strip the bark from the trees, but it is not a threatened species. Some certified lumber is available.

AVAILABILITY AND COST

Easy to buy and one of the cheapest temperate hardwoods, at nearly half the cost of oak or cherry.

Key uses	Interior Mass-produced furniture Bentwood furniture	Technical Workshop jigs
		Joinery Doweling and compressed biscuits Store interiors

Fraxinus americana
White ash

STRENGTHS
- Superb for bending
- Strong
- Distinctive grain pattern
- Interesting effects with stain
- Very little sapwood
- Few defects

WEAKNESSES
- Yellows with age
- Can tear and splinter
- Latewood and earlywood can be of contrasting hardness and workability

Weight Medium to heavy (41 lb./cu. ft.) (660 kg/cu. m)
Strength Good
Seasoning and stability Both fine, but watch out for end splits
Wastage Medium, depending on grain direction
Range of board widths Good
Range of board thicknesses Good
Durability Needs preservatives for external use; relatively resistant to insect attack.

BENDY WOOD FAVORED FOR TOOL HANDLES
Pale in color, ash is an important wood, not so much for its decorative value as for its strength and whippy nature. White ash is open-grained, with distinctive rows of tiny open pores that show up even when it is painted or heavily stained, though they are more pronounced on European ash (*F. excelsior*). White ash's good shock resistance has always made it popular for tool handles and sports equipment, but make sure you use straight-grained pieces, as ash can splinter where the grain curves away from a cut.

KEY CHARACTERISTICS
Type Temperate hardwood
Other names American white ash (U.K.)
Alternatives Common boxwood (*Buxus sempervirens*), hickory (*Carya* species)
Sources United States and Canada
Color White
Texture Coarse and open-grained
Grain Straight
Hardness Hard

IN THE WORKSHOP
The latewood particularly is hard, and your planer will chatter if you try to work against the grain. It is difficult to stop the grain from chipping where it curves around a knot. You will soon know if a blade needs sharpening: when the shavings turn to dust.

Milling Can chip, but the grain is rarely interlocking and is often straight, so you can usually find a way to cut and plane successfully.
Shaping Make shallow cuts, as the grain can tear if you try to remove too much stock in one go. Takes a good edge with sharp tools.
Assembly Will not bruise but will not give very much, so joints must be accurate. Can split. Distinctive grain pattern and range of color can make it difficult to hide joins if gluing up strips.
Finishing Takes most clear finishes well, but the hard patches do not take stain well.

VARIATIONS
Though olive coloring at the center is more common in European ash, you can find some rippled ash, especially as a veneer.

SUSTAINABILITY
Certified stocks are plentiful, but it is not under threat.

AVAILABILITY AND COST It is easy to find, and cost is relatively low for a hardwood, especially as wastage is not particularly high.

Key uses				
	Interior	Furniture		Luxury & leisure
		Stained office furniture		Sports equipment
	Marine	Boat building		Utility
				Tool handles

Fraxinus excelsior
European ash

STRENGTHS
- Strong, with excellent bending qualities
- Distinctive grain pattern
- Interesting effects with stain
- Very little sapwood
- Few defects

WEAKNESSES
- Pale color yellows
- Can tear and splinter
- Latewood and earlywood can be of contrasting hardness and workability

WHIPPY WOOD FROM A BENDY TREE
Often bent and distorted, the standing tree hints at the lumber's superb flexibility. The wood is pale in color, with distinctive rows of open pores that show up even when it is stained. Its good shock resistance has always made it popular for tool handles and sports equipment, but make sure you use straight-grained pieces.

KEY CHARACTERISTICS
Type Temperate hardwood
Other names Common ash
Alternatives Hickory (*Carya species*), English oak (*Quercus robur*), elm (*Ulmus hollandica* or *U. procera*)
Sources Europe
Color White
Texture Coarse and open-grained, but takes a sharp edge
Grain Straight
Hardness Hard
Weight Medium to heavy (44 lb./cu. ft.) (700 kg/cu. m)

Strength Good
Seasoning and stability Fine, but watch out for end splits
Wastage Medium, depending on grain direction
Range of board widths Good
Range of board thicknesses Good availability of all thicknesses
Durability Needs preservatives for external use. Relatively resistant to insect attack.

IN THE WORKSHOP
Ash takes an edge beautifully, but the curving grain can catch and splinter or tear. The latewood in particular is hard, and planing against the grain will cause the planer to stutter. Where the grain curves around a knot it can be very difficult to stop the grain chipping. If the shavings turn to dust your blade needs sharpening.

Milling Can chip, but the grain is rarely interlocking and tends to be straight, so you can usually find a way to cut and plane successfully.
Shaping Make shallow cuts, as the grain can tear if you try to remove too much stock in one go. Takes a good edge with sharp tools.
Assembly Will not bruise but will not give very much. Distinctive grain pattern and range of color can make it difficult to hide joins when planking up panels.
Finishing Takes most clear finishes well, but the hard patches sometimes appear case-hardened, and stains will not grip.

VARIATIONS
Olive coloring at the center is more common in European ash than white ash (*F. americana*). Some rippled ash is available, especially as veneer.

SUSTAINABILITY
Some certified stocks available, but it is under no threat.

AVAILABILITY AND COST
It is easy to find and cost is relatively low. Wastage is not particularly high, though watch out for end splits.

Key uses

Interior Furniture making Stained office furniture	**Utility** Tool handles
Marine Boat building	**Luxury & leisure** Sports equipment

Gossypiospermum praecox
Maracaibo boxwood

STRENGTHS
- Smooth, even texture
- Subtle grain pattern
- Hard and dense

WEAKNESSES
- Limited dimensions available
- Poor seasoning
- Hard to cut

BOXWOOD BY NATURE, IF NOT BY BOTANICAL NAME

Like many of the boxwoods that are not related to the *Buxus* species, Maracaibo boxwood is a beautiful wood to turn, as it has an almost creamy color and texture. Some wider stock is available, but generally boards are of limited width. The hardness and shock resistance of the lumber makes it popular for handles and other turned items.

KEY CHARACTERISTICS
Type Tropical hardwood
Other names *Casearia praecox*, castelo
Alternatives Common boxwood (*Buxus sempervirens*), jelutong (*Dyera costulata*), Kamassi boxwood (*Gonioma kamassi*), San Domingo boxwood (*Phyllostylon brasiliensis*)
Sources Venezuela, Colombia, West Indies
Color Yellow
Texture Even, fine and very smooth
Grain Close and generally straight
Hardness Hard

Weight Heavy (53 lb./cu. ft.) (850 kg/cu. m)
Strength Considered to have good shock resistance
Seasoning and stability Slow to season and prone to checking, but very stable once seasoned.
Wastage Likely to be moderate as sapwood is hardly noticeable, but if the dimensions are small a fair amount will be wasted in gluing up larger boards.
Range of board widths Likely to be limited
Range of board thicknesses Likely to be limited
Durability Good, but some risk of insects attacking sapwood

IN THE WORKSHOP
The creamy texture makes Maracaibo boxwood a joy to turn and to carve, but it is hard on tool edges.

Milling Surfaces well, as the grain is generally straight, but can chip.
Shaping Beautiful to turn and carve, and can be profiled accurately for sharp moldings. Like the true boxwoods, it is often used for chess pieces.
Assembly Should not move much and is not particularly oily, so gluing should be fine. Does not tend to split, but is hard enough for screws, and nails need pilot holes.
Finishing Finishes to a beautiful luster.

VARIATIONS
Watch out for blue staining if humidity is high. You can find rays and even some figuring on quartersawn surfaces. As a veneer, Maracaibo boxwood is sometimes stained black to imitate ebony.

SUSTAINABILITY
Not listed as being vulnerable, but no certified lumber found.

AVAILABILITY AND COST
Not widely available, but should not be particularly expensive when you do find it.

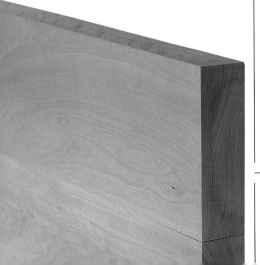

Key uses

Decorative
Turning
Decorative
veneering

Luxury & leisure
Precision and musical instruments

Technical
Printing and engraving blocks

Guaiacum officinale
Lignum-vitae

STRENGTHS
- Exquisite color and pattern
- Self-lubricating
- Extremely durable, hard and strong

WEAKNESSES
- Very limited supply
- Very expensive
- Very difficult to work

TREE OF LIFE, THREATENED WITH EXTINCTION

An extraordinary wood, lignum-vitae is not only beautiful but exceptionally heavy and strong, and remarkably durable. It has been overexploited for centuries and is now in short supply. Grown in the coastal regions of Central America, lignum-vitae (which translates as "tree of life") has been harvested for its medicinal resin and because its oily nature makes it self-lubricating – ideal for pulleys, bearings, wheels, rollers and die-cutting. It is used for balls in the game of bowls.

KEY CHARACTERISTICS
Type Tropical hardwood
Other names Ironwood, wood of life
Related species *G. sanctum* and *G. guatemalense*
Alternatives Greenheart (*Ocotea rodiaei*)
Sources Central America
Color Stripes of olive-green, dark yellow, tan, dark brown and black, with a flecked herringbone effect
Texture Generally fine and even, but can tear easily and feel coarse

Grain Interlocking and wavy
Hardness Very hard
Weight Very heavy (72–82 lb./cu. ft.) (1150–1310 kg/cu. m)
Strength Very strong
Seasoning and stability Must be seasoned carefully; moderate movement once dry
Wastage Few defects so wastage should not be high
Range of board widths Limited
Range of board thicknesses Likely to be limited
Durability Very durable, but some risk of insect attack

IN THE WORKSHOP
Lignum-vitae is difficult to work; it will chatter over cutters, and its oiliness can make it awkward to glue.

Milling Very tricky. The interlocking grain is liable to tear, and the wood jumps over cutters, though it will not dull them particularly. You need to make very fine cuts.
Shaping Will tear, especially on quartersawn sides, but is hard and will take a superb edge.
Assembly Screwing and nailing are difficult, and you will need to experiment with adhesives to find the best one.
Finishing Polishes to a superb finish.

VARIATIONS
On quartersawn sides the wood is striped, while plain-sawn faces reveal spectacular flamed grain and beautiful wavy bands.

SUSTAINABILITY
Lignum-vitae is listed on the CITES Appendix II, which means it must be used with great caution. The species is certainly endangered, and in some places extinct. The same is true for the very similar *G. sanctum*, which is often sold under the name lignum-vitae.

AVAILABILITY AND COST
It is sometimes available from suppliers specializing in exotics, but is very expensive. It is often sold by weight rather than by board.

Key uses

 Marine
Marine components

 Decorative
Turning

 Technical
Clock movements
Bearings and pulleys
Die-cutting

Guibourtia demeusei
Bubinga

STRENGTHS
- Hard and strong
- Distinctive figure
- Cheap rosewood

WEAKNESSES
- Swirling and interlocking grain
- Hard on tools
- Inconsistent coloring

HARD AND WILD-LOOKING, WITH DISTINCTIVE COLORING

Bubinga is initially pinky red but darkens with age, and it has an interesting brown-red figure, with a mixture of straight and interlocking grain. Irregular brown-red gum lines add to the intriguing color. Hard-wearing and with a fine finish, it is useful for solid wood flooring, and for tool handles as an alternative to rosewood.

KEY CHARACTERISTICS

Type Tropical hardwood
Other names African rosewood
Alternatives Louro (*Nectandra* species)
Sources Central and West Africa
Color Brown-red, with some purple streaking
Texture Coarse and open but consistent
Grain Sometimes straight but usually swirling; occasionally curved and interlocking
Hardness Hard
Weight Heavy, but moderate for a tropical hardwood (55 lb./cu. ft.) (880 kg/cu. m)
Strength Does not bend well, but neither does it bruise easily.

Seasoning and stability Seasons well; stable
Wastage Could be high, considering the inconsistent grain patterning and possible pockets of resin. There is a fair amount of pale sapwood.
Range of board widths May be limited
Range of board thicknesses May be limited
Durability Prone to insect attack, and only the sapwood will take preservative.

IN THE WORKSHOP

This is not a lumber for the faint-hearted, though the even texture makes machining relatively simple, whether or not the grain is interlocking. Make sure you use sharp tools. Bubinga is more commonly used as a veneer known as kevasingo, though workbenches have been made from it. Heavy and with flat surfaces, they have stood the test of time. This wood is certainly tough.

Milling Planes and cuts well enough, though abrasive on teeth and edges. Takes very thin passes. Check often for dulled edges.
Shaping Fine for routing and cutting joints, but make sure the grain is straight where joints are positioned.
Assembly Bubinga is stable, so there should be no problem with construction projects, and it glues well.
Finishing Comes up to a glowing brown with a fine surface finish.

VARIATIONS

The most notable special effect you can achieve with bubinga is to use the rotary-cut veneer kevasingo.

SUSTAINABILITY

I have not been able to find bubinga from a certified source, but it does not appear on the IUCN list of endangered species, nor in the CITES Appendices.

AVAILABILITY AND COST

Used for tool handles and furniture making, bubinga is likely to become more popular as supplies of rosewood diminish. Its price is moderate for a tropical hardwood.

Key uses

🏠 **Interior**
Furniture making
Flooring

⚙ **Technical**
Workbenches

▦ **Decorative**
Veneer for cabinetmaking

◢ **Utility**
Tool handles

Ilex opaca
American holly

STRENGTHS
- Creamy white color
- Fine, even texture
- Carves and turns well

WEAKNESSES
- Interlocking grain
- Available only in small dimensions
- Very limited supply

PURE WHITE TURNER'S WOOD

Use holly once and you will never forget it. Though it can be inconsistent in color, the most memorable lumber is pure white, with hardly any discernible grain pattern. However, this is hard to find. American holly has a fine, even texture and turns beautifully. For such a hard, tough wood, it is almost velvety to the touch, and sometimes it can have a green hue. Holly is not easy to use as there is often interlocking grain (which the turner will not notice) and it can dull tools. The lumber is not very stable, it seasons poorly and dimensions are usually limited by the smallness of the tree. Though it is not durable, American holly is unlikely to be used for purposes where that would matter. Stained black it is often used as a substitute for ebony.

KEY CHARACTERISTICS

Type Hardwood
Related species *I. aquifolium*
Sources *I. opaca* is grown in the United States, but there are many species of holly around the world.
Color Creamy white
Texture Fine and uniform, with a satiny feel
Grain Wavy and interlocking
Hardness Hard and tough
Weight Heavy (50 lb./cu. ft.) (800 kg/cu. m)

AVAILABILITY AND SUSTAINABILITY

Few American hollies are felled because there is such a high demand for berries and leaves, so the most likely sources are local tree surgeons, specialist turning and carving suppliers, and veneer dealers. There is not much American holly on the commercial market, and none that is certified, but the species is under no threat.

Key uses

Decorative
Turning
Inlay and stringing

Luxury & leisure
Musical instruments
Chess pieces

Juglans cinerea
Butternut

STRENGTHS
- Good grain pattern
- Interesting color
- Widely available and economical

WEAKNESSES
- Soft and weak
- Moves moderately once dry
- Not durable

A WALNUT IN ALL BUT COLOR

Butternut shares the texture, weight and grain of black walnut (*J. nigra*), but is far paler, with distinct latewood lines. The tree tends to grow away from woods or forests along the east coast of North America. It is not particularly large, never exceeding 100 feet in height and 3 feet in diameter. The sweet nuts are used for making candies.

KEY CHARACTERISTICS

Type Temperate hardwood
Other names White walnut
Sources Eastern North America
Color Sapwood is light brown or beige; the darker heartwood has reddish latewood lines
Texture Medium to coarse, but even
Grain Straight
Hardness Soft
Weight Light (28 lb./cu. ft.) (450 kg/cu. m)

IN THE WORKSHOP

With a straight grain, butternut works well. It takes a good edge and will not dull tools, but it may tear if tools are not sharp. Butternut can be polished to a good luster and takes stain well.

AVAILABILITY AND SUSTAINABILITY

In plentiful supply, but even so, certified lumber is available. Cost is moderate.

Key uses **Interior** Furniture

Joinery Interior trim

Decorative Carving

Juglans nigra
Black walnut

STRENGTHS

- Widely available and cost-effective
- Good substitute for more expensive dark woods
- Straight-grained and easy to use
- Finishes beautifully
- Interesting color and texture

WEAKNESSES

- Dusty to machine, with an unpleasant odor
- Causes some dulling of cutting edges
- Finishes can mist
- Coarse texture
- Soft, and bruises easily

VERSATILE HARDWOOD THAT IS DARK IN COLOR AND LIGHT IN WEIGHT

Once considered a poor relative of English walnut (*J. regia*), black walnut is now a popular lumber worldwide for furniture and cabinetmaking, and for specialist work on clocks, carvings and gunstocks. Grown across North America, the lumber is usually straight-grained, with streaky dark brown heartwood that can have a purple hue. It is usually supplied kiln-dried and feels remarkably lightweight for a hardwood.

KEY CHARACTERISTICS

Type Temperate hardwood
Other names American black walnut (U.K.)
Alternatives Brown oak, which is the diseased form of English oak (*Quercus robur*)
Sources U.S. and Canada

Color Dark brown with some lighter streaks, fading toward the edges with a faint purple hue
Texture Even, but slightly coarse
Grain Generally straight, but can be wavy
Hardness Soft to medium for a hardwood
Weight Medium to heavy (40 lb./cu. ft.) (640 kg/cu. m)
Strength Medium, but can bruise easily
Seasoning and stability Stable; seasons reasonably well but can check and degrade if dried too quickly.
Wastage Low
Range of board widths Good
Range of board thicknesses Good
Durability Moderate; needs preservative for external use.

IN THE WORKSHOP

Very easy to use, with little wastage because the sapwood is very thin. Black walnut is easily worked with machine and hand tools, and takes a sharp edge from cutters. Can be very dusty, and some woodworkers find the distinctive odor unpleasant and irritating.

Milling Good finish from saws, jointers and planers.
Shaping Routs beautifully, with moderate dulling.
Assembly Fine for gluing, but can be dusty, so needs some care. Glue can easily soak into the grain and be difficult to remove. Good stability after assembly.
Finishing Finishes to a beautiful shine and takes most polishes well. A milky mist can appear after finishing, especially if you use shellac.

VARIATIONS

Some veneer is available, mainly for decorative effects. Some boards may have a little rippled figure.

SUSTAINABILITY

Black walnut is widely available from certified sustainable sources. It should be under no threat.

AVAILABILITY AND COST

It is easy to find at hardwood suppliers. Very low wastage rates make black walnut a good value.

Key uses

Interior Furniture and cabinetmaking

Joinery Interior joinery

Marine Boat building

Luxury & leisure Gunstocks Musical instruments

Decorative Carving

Juglans regia
English walnut

STRENGTHS
- Incomparable grain
- Wide color range
- Easy to use

WEAKNESSES
- Expensive
- High wastage
- Vulnerable to insect attack

HARDWOOD THAT IS MUCH MIMICKED BUT NEVER MATCHED

English walnut has an extraordinary color range and the most subtle and intriguing grain patterning, characterized by gentle undulating curves. The species is easy to use, but the lumber is very expensive, the sapwood is wide and wastage is high. Furniture makers are known to buy fallen trees on the spot, for either veneer or solid lumber, in the hope that there is something they can use.

KEY CHARACTERISTICS
Type Temperate hardwood
Other names European walnut, Persian walnut
Related species Japanese walnut (*J. ailantifolia*)
Alternatives Black walnut (*J. nigra*), Brazilian rosewood (*Dalbergia nigra*)
Sources Europe and parts of Asia
Color From gray and beige through pink to brown
Texture Fine and even
Grain Curving or straight, but not interlocking
Hardness Medium
Weight Medium to heavy (40 lb./cu. ft.) (640 kg/cu. m)

Strength Moderate, but bends well
Seasoning and stability Easy to season, though it must be done slowly. Will move moderately once dry.
Wastage High
Range of board widths Can be wide, but often limited because logs are not always very wide and there can be a high proportion of sapwood.
Range of board thicknesses Reasonable, though walnut is sometimes cut thick when it is not sliced for veneer for later flexibility.
Durability Moderate, but some risk of insect attack

IN THE WORKSHOP

English walnut is one of the easiest of woods to work – it carves and turns beautifully and is easy to prepare, glue and finish. If only more walnut trees were grown!

Milling It takes some time to cut away the sapwood, as it can be intrusive, but it is worth being economical and saving all the good heartwood, which planes or surfaces very well, with only a slight tendency to tear. The lumber will chip only around knots.
Shaping Takes a superb edge.
Assembly Glues, nails and screws well, with no need for pre-drilling.
Finishing Will take any finish and has a soft luster.

VARIATIONS

Crotch and burl walnut are the most common special veneers, but a pale version can also be found. Ancona walnut, from Italy, is highly figured.

SUSTAINABILITY

There are plenty of walnut trees growing, but most are not old enough to harvest and many die before they grow to a valuable size. As a result you will not find certified English walnut, but there is no risk of extinction.

AVAILABILITY AND COST

English walnut is difficult to find and usually expensive.

Key uses

Interior
Furniture
Cabinetmaking

Decorative
Turning
Carving
Veneer for paneling

Utility
Boxmaking

Kunzea ericoides
Kunzea

STRENGTHS
- Strong and durable
- Substitute for teak

WEAKNESSES
- Difficult to source

KIWI LUMBER OF GREAT BEAUTY

It is said that Captain Cook, the great British explorer, was the first person to brew tea from the leaves of kanuka, which is also known as kunzea. It is a relatively small tree and the lumber is tough, with a gnarled look. It was formerly used for beaters, paddles, weapons, blades and wheel spokes. Today it is converted into charcoal, but it is also a fine lumber with fairly straight grain and is both durable and strong. It has some similarities to teak (*Tectona grandis*) or English oak (*Quercus robur*).

KEY CHARACTERISTICS
Type Temperate hardwood
Other names Kanuka, manuka, *K. ericifolia*
Sources New Zealand
Color Rich mid- to dark brown, with darker streaks and some evidence of gum pockets
Texture Fine, but not entirely uniform
Grain Generally straight
Hardness Medium hard with reasonable luster
Weight Medium to heavy (45 lb./cu. ft.) (720 kg/cu. m)

AVAILABILITY AND SUSTAINABILITY
Not a wood exploited for its lumber, and essential for the harvest of its leaves, so any wood available was probably ready for felling and probably replaced. It isn't easy to find, but won't be particularly expensive to buy.

Key uses
 Interior Furniture

Joinery Interior trim

 Technical Wheel components

Utility Handles

Laburnum anagyroides
Laburnum

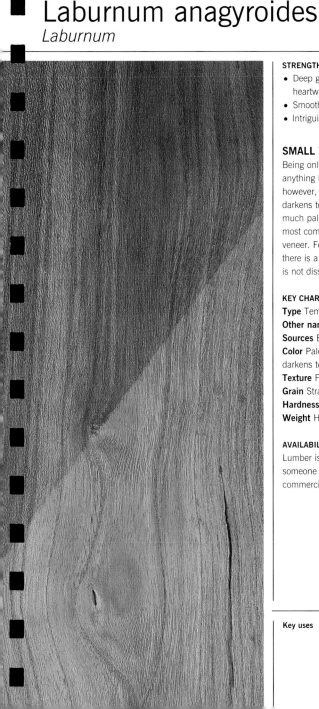

STRENGTHS
- Deep golden-brown heartwood
- Smooth, fine texture
- Intriguing grain pattern

WEAKNESSES
- Available only in small dimensions
- Liable to check and split

SMALL TREE THAT BEARS OYSTERS

Being only a small tree, laburnum is rarely available in anything but small dimensions. It is worth seeking out, however, for its distinctive heartwood, which quickly darkens to a golden brown, while the sapwood remains much paler. The heartwood can be used for turning but is most commonly cut across the grain to be used as oyster veneer. For that reason it has to be seasoned carefully as there is a risk of end splits and checks. The grain pattern is not dissimilar to that of wenge (*Millettia laurentii*).

KEY CHARACTERISTICS

Type Temperate hardwood
Other names Golden chain tree
Sources Europe
Color Pale sapwood, with yellowy green heartwood that darkens to a golden brown
Texture Fine to medium, but even
Grain Straight
Hardness Medium to hard
Weight Heavy (52 lb./cu. ft.) (830 kg/cu. m)

AVAILABILITY AND SUSTAINABILITY

Lumber is generally available only as a veneer, or from someone who is felling a laburnum tree. There is little commercial demand for the lumber.

Key uses

Interior
Cabinet and furniture making

Joinery
Interior joinery

Luxury & leisure
Gunstocks

Larix decidua
European larch

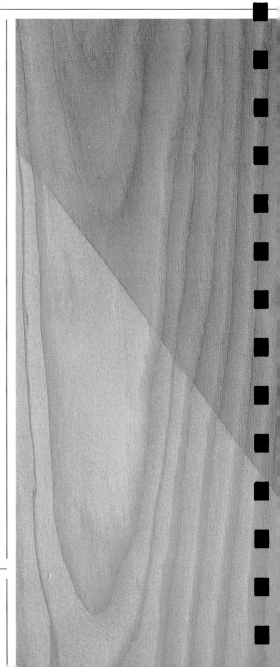

STRENGTHS
- Durability and toughness
- Straight grain and even texture
- Distinctive grain pattern

WEAKNESSES
- Knots
- Tendency to split

EVENLY STRIPED SOFTWOOD WITH MANY RELATIVES

Like many softwoods, European larch is characterized by large annular rings, with dark red-brown latewood bands. However, the texture is more even than in some softwoods, and the lumber is harder and stronger, so it is preferred for some joinery and for structural uses. It was often the wood of choice for telephone poles and pit props used in mines. Woodworkers need to look out for knots and for splitting.

KEY CHARACTERISTICS
Type Temperate softwood
Other names *L. europaea*
Similar species Western larch (*L. occidentalis*), tamarack larch (*L. laricina*), Siberian larch (*L. russica* or *L. sibirica*), Japanese larch (*L. kaempferi* or *L. leptolepis*)
Sources Europe
Color Alternating bands of light brown and darker reddish brown, with an overall orange-red hue
Texture Evenly fine
Grain Straight
Hardness Hard for a softwood
Weight Medium, but relatively heavy for a softwood (37 lb./cu. ft.) (590 kg/cu. m)

AVAILABILITY AND SUSTAINABILITY
Available in Europe from certified sources, which does ensure some degree of biodiversity for softwood forests. Even so, European larch is not endangered and the lumber is safe to use. Cost is moderate.

Key uses

↗ **Construction**
Building
Pit props
Telephone poles

⌐ **Joinery**
External joinery

Larix occidentalis
Western larch

STRENGTHS
- Straight grain
- Moderate price

WEAKNESSES
- Splits easily
- Difficult to season

SUPERB LARCH THAT COULD BE A FIR

Often confused with Douglas fir (*Pseudotsuga menziesii*), which is very similar, western larch is used mainly for building. It is ideal for this purpose because the grain is generally straight, there are few defects and the lumber is reasonably durable, especially when treated with preservative. The main problem is that it splits easily, which makes it difficult to nail, but it glues and screws well. Its fibrous nature can also make it awkward to work.

KEY CHARACTERISTICS
Type Temperate softwood
Other names Larch, western tamarack, hackmatack, mountain larch
Related species Tamarack larch (*L. laricina*), Siberian larch (*L. sibirica*)
Sources Northwest United States and Canada
Color Narrow, pale sapwood and red-brown heartwood
Texture Relatively coarse for a softwood, with significant contrast between the pale earlywood and darker latewood lines
Grain Straight, with the growth rings very close together
Hardness Soft to medium and moderately durable
Weight Medium (36 lb./cu. ft.) (580 kg/cu. m)

AVAILABILITY AND SUSTAINABILITY
Widely available and not listed as threatened. Certified supplies are available.

Key uses **Construction**
Telephone poles
Joinery
Interior trim

Liriodendron tulipifera
Tuliptree

STRENGTHS
- Fine, even texture
- Straight grain
- Lightweight utility lumber
- Honey coloring

WEAKNESSES
- Not durable
- Soft and fibrous
- Sapwood prone to insect attack

UTILITY HARDWOOD THAT SURPASSES MANY SOFTWOODS

Many woodworkers get used to working with hardwoods, but recognize there are times when a hidden carcass or framework can be made from a secondary lumber. That is when tuliptree, with a fine, consistent texture and relatively low price, comes into its own.

KEY CHARACTERISTICS
Type Temperate hardwood
Other names American whitewood, tulip poplar
Alternatives Kauri (*Agathis* species), red alder (*Alnus rubra*), paraná pine (*Araucaria angustifolia*), hoop pine (*Araucaria cunninghamii*), paper birch (*Betula papyrifera*)
Sources North America and Europe
Color Creamy white with green, brown, red and even blue streaks that darken with age to honey brown
Texture Even and fine
Grain Straight
Hardness Soft and fibrous
Weight Medium (31 lb./cu. ft.) (500 kg/cu. m)
Strength Medium

Seasoning and stability Sapwood can be very wide. Seasons well and quickly without damage, and continues to be stable in use.
Wastage High if you are looking for lumber that is clear of colored streaks or sapwood, but otherwise low for this utility species.
Range of board widths Good
Range of board thicknesses Good
Durability Poor. Sapwood prone to insect attack. Not durable outside unless treated with preservative (which it takes well). However, do not let it touch the ground as it will decay.

IN THE WORKSHOP
Many woodworkers regard tuliptree as nothing more than a utility hardwood that is on the soft side. Easy to cut and plane, it glues well and is forgiving. It is more stable than many softwoods and does not suffer from a contrast between earlywood and latewood.

Milling Easy. Flattens nicely and does not move.
Shaping Not hard enough to take a complicated profile with the same precision as harder lumber, but corners are sharp and joint-cutting is simple.
Assembly Takes glue well, and softness offers some tolerance.
Finishing Finishes well, with a reasonable luster for such a soft hardwood. Needs sanding after planing, as tools will raise some fibers.

VARIATIONS
Used for plywood.

SUSTAINABILITY
A good species to encourage, as it grows rapidly. Unthreatened.

AVAILABILITY AND COST
Tuliptree is an inexpensive hardwood that is relatively easy to find, and which competes favorably in hardness, stability and strength with many softwoods.

Key uses

Decorative Carving and patternmaking

Joinery General joinery

Interior Doors

Luxury & leisure Toys

Lovoa trichilioides
African tigerwood

STRENGTHS
- Inexpensive
- Substitute for walnut or mahogany

WEAKNESSES
- Mediocre strength and durability
- Possibly endangered
- Limited availability

MAHOGANY THAT RESEMBLES WALNUT
Known by some woodworkers as striped or African walnut, this species does not have the even patterning of zebrawood, but it does possess an intriguing color and grain. It is part of the mahogany (Meliaceae) family rather than a walnut (Juglandaceae). Irregular thin, dark lines intersperse gradual changes in color from light to dark honey, with some yellowish patches. Once finished it shimmers like a hologram, with colors altering as you move the lumber in light. The thin black lines on crown-cut or quartersawn lumber can be used creatively.

KEY CHARACTERISTICS
Type Tropical hardwood
Other names Striped walnut (U.K.), African walnut (U.K.)
Alternatives English walnut (*Juglans regia*), mahogany (*Swietenia* species), snakewood (*Piratinera guianensis*)
Sources Central and West Africa
Color From yellow-tan to rich dark honey
Texture Varies, but moderately open
Grain Often interlocking in small patches, but generally straight or gently curving
Hardness Moderate

Weight Medium (35 lb./cu. ft.) (560 kg/cu. m)
Strength Mediocre for a hardwood
Seasoning and stability Seasons well, but has a tendency to split if there is heart shake. Moderate movement once seasoned.
Wastage Low
Range of board widths Varies greatly from yard to yard, but can be wide.
Range of board thicknesses Limited, but thick boards are available.
Durability Has some resistance to pests and rot.

IN THE WORKSHOP
Tigerwood is, as many of its characteristics indicate, a fairly average lumber, used more often for economy than for effect. It can be employed as a substitute for English walnut (*Juglans regia*) or for aged mahogany, at least for inconspicuous components. It is not hard to use, though it has some interlocking grain.

Milling Fine, but take shallow cuts when there is interlocking grain, or reduce the cutting angle.
Shaping Can be routed or turned easily, though it is on the dusty side.
Assembly Takes glue well and won't move much.
Finishing Good; takes any finish well.

VARIATIONS
Quartersawn lumber has subtle lines that can produce an attractive figure.

SUSTAINABILITY
Tigerwood has been listed as vulnerable in some African countries by IUCN. There are few signs of certified supplies.

AVAILABILITY AND COST
African tigerwood is imported by some specialist dealers, in varying widths and thicknesses, and is only a little more expensive than some softwoods.

Key uses

Utility
Utility furniture

Interior
Flooring

Decorative
Veneer for paneling
Turning

Luxury & leisure
Gunstocks

Magnolia grandifolia
Southern magnolia

STRENGTHS
- Stable and easy to work
- Consistent texture
- Straight grain

WEAKNESSES
- Bland
- Not widely available
- Some mineral streaking

STABLE HARDWOOD WITH TINGE OF GREEN

The state tree of Mississippi, the southern magnolia is particularly stable and can be machined easily and accurately, which makes it ideal for the production of venetian blind slats, louvers and moldings. Otherwise it is used as a utility lumber and sometimes for furniture and cabinetmaking, as it is easy to use and finish. It seasons well but is not durable. Logs exhibiting mineral streaks are often sliced into decorative veneer. Magnolia is quite similar in appearance and use to tuliptree (*Liriodendron tulipifera*), but a little harder and more consistent in color.

KEY CHARACTERISTICS

Type Temperate hardwood
Other names Magnolia, bat tree, big laurel, bullbay, great laurel magnolia, mountain magnolia, evergreen magnolia
Related species *M. virginiana*
Sources United States
Color Pale tan or straw, with greenish hue and occasional purple streaks; narrow yellow sapwood
Texture Uniformly medium
Grain Straight
Hardness Fairly hard, and relatively strong
Weight Medium (35 lb./cu. ft.) (560 kg/cu. m)

AVAILABILITY AND SUSTAINABILITY

Magnolia is not expensive, but is more readily available through wholesalers for mass production than through retail outlets. It does not appear to be vulnerable, and we have not found certified supplies.

Key uses **Decorative** Thin slats and moldings

Joinery Interior trim

Interior Flooring Mass-produced furniture

Malus sylvestris
Apple

STRENGTHS
- Fruitwood coloring

WEAKNESSES
- Brittle
- Unstable
- Tough on tools

LESSER OF THE FRUITWOODS

Some of the fruitwood species, particularly cherry (*Prunus serotina* and *P. avium*) and pearwood (*Pyrus communis*), are silky smooth and have subtle pattern and color. Though it has something of the same coloring, apple does not match up to these species in many respects. The patterning and color are indistinct, and though it is a hard lumber, it often feels a bit woolly. It dulls tools, is hard to work, is not particularly stable and seasons poorly. Apple is, however, interesting to carve and turn. The wavy grain and hardness make it suitable for tool handles, but it is too brittle for bending.

KEY CHARACTERISTICS

Type Temperate hardwood
Other names Crabapple
Related species Hupeh apple (*M. hupehensis*), Japanese crabapple (*M. floribunda*), *M. pumila*, *Pyrus malus*
Sources United States, Europe, southwest Asia
Color Pale tan to pink, with variable darker streaks and little distinction between heartwood and sapwood
Texture Fine and even
Grain Wavy
Hardness Hard
Weight Medium to heavy (45 lb./cu. ft.) (720 kg/cu. m)

AVAILABILITY AND SUSTAINABILITY

Apple is not easy to buy, and is most commonly obtained from local orchards rather than through lumberyards or even specialist suppliers. Some veneer and turning blanks are available. Apple is under no threat, but it is not sufficiently commercial to warrant certification.

Key uses **Decorative**
Turning
Carving
Veneer

 Utility
Tool handles

Metopium brownii
Chechen

STRENGTHS

- Hard and heavy
- Stripy grain pattern
- Deep reddish brown color

WEAKNESSES

- Tendency to tear
- Limited availability

WALNUT SUBSTITUTE WITH NOXIOUS BARK

Chechen is a beautiful lumber in the style of an aged mahogany, being dark reddish brown with a wavy, striped grain. The tree, which can grow up to 50 feet high, grows in Central America and particularly Mexico, but has probably been saved from exploitation by the poisonous bark and sap. The toxins have the same effect as poison ivy. Fortunately the wood itself is not poisonous.

KEY CHARACTERISTICS

Type Tropical hardwood
Other names Honduras walnut (U.K.), *chechen nigro*, black chechen, black poison wood, chechem
Alternatives Brazilian rosewood (*Dalbergia nigra*), though this is very difficult to find and is vulnerable to extinction.
Sources Central America and Mexico
Color Dark and deep reddish brown, with lighter and darker stripes
Texture Fine to medium
Grain Straight, with a gentle wave, and likely to have some interlocking grain
Hardness Hard

Weight Heavy (53 lb./cu. ft.) (850 kg/cu. m)
Strength Strong
Seasoning and stability Seemingly good to season and stable once dry
Wastage Low. Few imperfections, but there is contrasting yellow sapwood.
Range of board widths Variable
Range of board thicknesses Variable
Durability Used for construction work in Central America, so it must have some natural durability.

IN THE WORKSHOP

Chechen is not used commonly because it has not been harvested and processed on a commercial scale so little is known about its qualities. It looks as though it could be tricky to work, but it actually cuts and planes well. The dust is not thought to be poisonous like the bark, which can cause inflammation.

Milling Planing well, with some tendency to chip. The wood is hard but does not dull tools.
Shaping Takes a good profile and is easy to work, as the texture is fine and even.
Assembly Good. Glues well, though nails and screws may need pre-drilling.
Finishing Polishes to a high luster.

VARIATIONS

The plain-sawn sides have a marvelous grain pattern, and this, combined with the rich red-brown color, makes the lumber resemble a rosewood.

SUSTAINABILITY

Certified supplies are now available. This is the sort of lesser-known species that woodworkers should be encouraged to use, from certified sources, to stimulate demand for abundant tropical species.

AVAILABILITY AND COST

Moderately priced, but you may have to search to find it from a specialist in exotic hardwoods.

Key uses **Interior** Furniture Cabinetmaking   **Decorative** Turning   **Luxury & leisure** Musical instruments

Microberlinia brazzavillensis
Zebrawood

STRENGTHS
- Stripy figure
- Good finish
- Hard, heavy and stable
- Available as veneer

WEAKNESSES
- Can be expensive
- Veneer buckles
- Constrasting density of bands

TROPICAL HARDWOOD WITH DISTINCTIVE STRIPES

It should come as no surprise that what is known as zebrano in Europe has come to be called zebrawood in the United States. The light, dark and medium brown stripes are largely straight on quartersawn sides, but often beautifully wavy on crown-cut faces or edges. Unfortunately, the lines vary in density as well as color, and the interlocking grain makes working awkward.

KEY CHARACTERISTICS
Type Tropical hardwood
Other names Zebrano (Europe)
Related species *M. bisulcata*
Alternatives Beli (*Paraberlinia bifoliolata*)
Sources West Africa
Color Dark brown-black lines interspersed with light and medium brown bands
Texture Moderately coarse and not particularly even
Grain Looks straight, but often interlocking and wavy
Hardness Varies between light and dark bands

Weight Medium to heavy (46 lb./cu. ft.) (740 kg/cu. m)
Strength Good
Seasoning and stability Can distort and check, but stable once seasoned.
Wastage Low
Range of board widths Variable
Range of board thicknesses Depends on stock, which is likely to be limited.
Durability Good

IN THE WORKSHOP

The contrasting bands of dark and light grain can be of varying density, which can make zebrawood a troublesome lumber to work with, though it is otherwise fine.

Milling Resort to sanding if the planer keeps picking up the grain.
Shaping Takes a good edge.
Assembly Take care gluing, and do a trial first. Very little movement to consider.
Finishing Needs a lot of sanding, but has a good luster.

VARIATIONS

The most common use for zebrawood is as a quartersawn veneer to display the straight lines. Make sure you keep the veneer weighted down, as it has a tendency to buckle.

SUSTAINABILITY

Zebrawood has been listed as potentially vulnerable by IUCN. Using zebrawood veneer is at least more efficient than using the wood in the solid, especially if you can fix it to a core made from a certified lumber.

AVAILABILITY AND COST

Fairly easy to obtain from specialist dealers in exotic hardwoods, but stock is likely to be limited in width and thickness. Prices vary and it may not be as expensive as you might expect.

Key uses	Decorative
	Bandings for decorative effects
	Turning
	Carving
	Marquetry
	Veneer

Millettia laurentii
Wenge

STRENGTHS	WEAKNESSES
• Hard and strong	• Not the easiest wood to finish
• Distinctive grain pattern	• Coarse texture
• Strong color	• Risk of checking during seasoning

DRAMATIC HARDWOOD THAT IS BEST LEFT UNFINISHED

Wenge is an unusual lumber, being very coarse but even in texture and very strong. It is favored for flooring and sometimes used for work surfaces. Closely related to panga panga (*M. stuhlmannii*), it is distinguished by its straight grain and alternating dark brown and paler veins, which give it a special look and feel. It is rather more dramatic unfinished, as the alternating veins converge in color when a finish is applied.

KEY CHARACTERISTICS

Type Tropical hardwood
Other names Dikela, kiboto, pallisandre
Alternatives Panga panga (*M. stuhlmannii*)
Sources Central Africa
Color Dark brown, with paler veins that darken when finished
Texture Coarse, but even
Grain Generally straight
Hardness Very hard
Weight Heavy (55 lb./cu. ft.) (880 kg/cu. m)

Strength Very strong, and can be bent
Seasoning and stability Stable once dry, but must be seasoned slowly to prevent degradation.
Wastage Medium, with some sapwood and gum pockets, but otherwise few defects
Range of board widths Good
Range of board thicknesses Should be reasonable
Durability Very durable to rot and insect attack

IN THE WORKSHOP

Wenge might be expected to be very difficult to use, as the grain pattern indicates a tendency to splinter. In fact that is not the case, and the lumber is used extensively by furniture makers and for flooring.

Milling Planes very well to a beautiful smooth finish.
Shaping Being coarse, wenge is always at risk of tearing, and you cannot expect edges to be perfectly sharp. However, the texture is even and the wood is hard.
Assembly Wenge does not nail well and it needs pre-drilling, as is also the case for screws. There should be no problems with glue.
Finishing Finishes can be inconsistent because the permeability of the veins can vary.

VARIATIONS

There is very little contrast between quartersawn and plain-sawn sides.

SUSTAINABILITY

Wenge has been reported to be endangered by IUCN and there is no evidence of certified supplies.

AVAILABILITY AND COST

More expensive than panga panga (*M. stuhlmannii*) but still moderately priced for a tropical hardwood, wenge is not widely available, but it is increasingly popular for flooring, and that may be the easiest way to access supplies.

Key uses **Interior**
Furniture
Flooring
Work surfaces

Nothofagus cunninghamii
Tasmanian myrtle

STRENGTHS
- Lovely red color
- Smooth, even texture
- Versatile

WEAKNESSES
- Interlocking grain
- Poor stability

VERSATILE PINK HARDWOOD

Very similar to the other great Australian hardwood, jarrah (*Eucalyptus marginata*), myrtle has a reddish color that darkens with age, and a smooth, even surface that can exhibit interesting figure and a little mottling from medullary rays. It is relatively easy to use, though there is some interlocking grain and some evidence of a little movement. Make sure you experiment with glue before assembly, but screwing and nailing should be fine. It is a versatile lumber, with the advantage of intriguing color and subtle grain pattern with good luster.

KEY CHARACTERISTICS

Type Temperate hardwood
Other names Tasmanian beech, Australian beech, myrtle beech
Similar species Jarrah (*Eucalyptus marginata*)
Sources Australia
Color Light red-brown that darkens with age, with narrow, pale sapwood
Texture Fine and even with a good luster
Grain Straight or wavy, but with some interlocking grain and some risk of knots and defects
Hardness Medium to hard
Weight Medium to heavy (45 lb./cu. ft.) (720 kg/cu. m)

AVAILABILITY AND SUSTAINABILITY

Little Tasmanian myrtle is exported to North America, and the price is likely to be medium to high. It does not appear to be endangered.

Key uses   **Interior** Furniture and cabinetmaking   **Decorative** Turning

Joinery Interior trim

Nothofagus menziesii
New Zealand silver beech

STRENGTHS
- Straight grained
- Fine, even texture

WEAKNESSES
- Nondurable
- Prone to insect attack
- Resists preservatives

BEECH FROM NEW ZEALAND

New Zealand silver beech is one of three *Nothofagus* species that populate New Zealand, along with red beech (*N. fusca*) and hard or clinker beech (*N. truncata*). None of them is a true beech (*Fagus* species). The wood dries fairly easily and distortion is relatively slight, though there is small movement in service. Silver beech works easily with both hand and machine tools, except where irregular grain is present on quartersawn stock, when a reduction in the cutting angle is recommended. Logs can be rotary cut for plywood and sliced for decorative veneers for furniture and paneling. These beeches stain and glue well and can be brought to a good finish, but they do not take preservative too well. Red and hard beech are both durable, but silver beech is not. They are all prone to attack by insects.

KEY CHARACTERISTICS

Type Temperate hardwood
Other names Southland beech
Related species *N. fusca* (red beech), *N. truncata* (hard beech, clinker beech)
Sources New Zealand
Color Inner heartwood is a uniform pink-brown in color
Texture Fine and even
Grain Straight, but sometimes curly
Hardness Medium
Weight Medium (33 lb./cu. ft.) (530 kg/cu. m)

AVAILABILITY AND SUSTAINABILITY

Silver beech is not widely available outside New Zealand, where the cutting of old forests is restricted. There is no indication of the species being under threat, and FSC silver beech is being produced.

Key uses

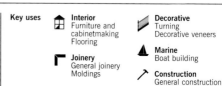

Interior
Furniture and cabinetmaking
Flooring

Joinery
General joinery
Moldings

Decorative
Turning
Decorative veneers

Marine
Boat building

Construction
General construction

Ochroma pyramidale
Balsa wood

STRENGTHS
- Extremely lightweight
- Easy to cut with a knife
- Buoyant
- Very strong relative to weight

WEAKNESSES
- Weak and brittle
- Bland grain pattern and color
- Expensive

A MODEL LUMBER DERIVED FROM SAPWOOD

Balsa wood is one of the few species that is commercially exploited for its sapwood. Its key qualities are buoyancy and ease of use for modelmaking. Balsa trees grow very fast, reaching 60 feet in only five years, but the tree and the lumber are very susceptible to damage.

KEY CHARACTERISTICS

Type Tropical hardwood
Other names *O. lagopus*, *O. bicolor* and corkwood
Sources West Indies, Central America, Ecuador
Color Beige with a pinkish hue
Texture Medium to coarse and even
Grain No obvious grain
Hardness Extremely soft
Weight Very light (10 lb./cu. ft.) (160 kg/cu. m)
Strength Weak and brittle, but strong for its weight

Seasoning and stability Difficult to season as it is so full of moisture initially, and though it has to be dried quickly it must not be overheated. Stable once dry.
Wastage Used with care, wastage should be low. There are few defects, and commercially available balsa wood is usually of good quality. Beware of crushing.
Range of board widths Good
Range of board thicknesses Good
Durability Poor

IN THE WORKSHOP

Balsa wood carves beautifully, as long as tools are sharp enough not to crush the fibers, and there is hardly any discernible grain to tear or chip.

Milling Edges must be sharp or the surface will be woolly.
Shaping As long as you manage to avoid crushing the fibers, you can cut a sharp edge, but the edges are usually vulnerable to bruising.
Assembly Glues well, but does not take nails or screws. It is, at least, very stable.
Finishing Some say that balsa has a high luster, but you have to work hard to get a good finish.

VARIATIONS

The heartwood is a pale brown, but is rarely used.

SUSTAINABILITY

There is no evidence that balsa wood is endangered.

AVAILABILITY AND COST

Balsa wood is sold in small quantities and is widely available in model stores. It is expensive compared to other lumber.

Key uses				
	▲	**Marine** Buoyancy	▨	**Decorative** Carving
	⚙	**Technical** Bearings and pulleys	⊶	**Luxury & leisure** Modelmaking

Ocotea rodiaei
Greenheart

STRENGTHS
- Dense, hard and strong
- Very durable in water

WEAKNESSES
- Poor seasoning and stability
- Difficult to use
- Toxic

HARD AND HEAVY MARINE LUMBER

Greenheart is not a particularly attractive lumber, and is valued mainly for its amazing natural durability and hardness. It is often the first choice for marine construction, particularly of boats and decking and is also used for bridges and jetties. Greenheart is difficult to work, but is amazingly strong. It is used in situations where poor seasoning is not an issue – underwater, for instance – where it doesn't matter if the surfaces are not perfect.

KEY CHARACTERISTICS
Type Tropical hardwood
Alternatives Lignum vitae (*Guaiacum officinale*)
Sources Guyana and Venezuela
Color Green, yellow, dark brown or olive
Texture Fine and even
Grain Straight or interlocking
Hardness Very hard
Weight Very heavy (64 lb./cu. ft.) (1020 kg/cu. m)
Strength Extremely strong

Seasoning and stability Slow to season, with a risk of splitting, and moves moderately once dry.
Wastage For fine work, wastage may be high, with a likelihood of checks and defects. These may be of less importance if the lumber is to be used for utility marine functions.
Range of board widths Moderate, depending on availability
Range of board thicknesses Fair, according to availability
Durability Extremely durable

IN THE WORKSHOP

Not an easy lumber to work. The only real benefit, other than its durability, is that the surface can be brought up to a wonderfully smooth finish, but it will take some effort to achieve this.

Milling Will blunt tools, and the grain is interlocking, so there is a risk of tearing.
Shaping Greenheart is known to splinter easily, and care must be taken, as the splinters can be poisonous.
Assembly Hard on screws and nails, which need to be pre-drilled. Experiment with glue bonds first to find the best results.
Finishing Good luster, and the smooth surface polishes well.

VARIATIONS

Some woods, such as English walnut, always have different shades or tones while others are more inconsistent in their color range. Greenheart can vary greatly in color, but its variation is not consistent.

SUSTAINABILITY

Some certified greenheart is available.

AVAILABILITY AND COST

Not widely available, as greenheart is not considered a woodworker's lumber, but it can be found through specialist importers and in specialist lumberyards.

Key uses			
▲ **Marine** Marine building Boat building		↗ **Construction** General construction	
▥ **Interior** Flooring		▥ **Exterior** Decking	

Paraberlinia bifoliolata
Beli

STRENGTHS
- Dramatic pattern
- Substitute for zebrawood

WEAKNESSES
- Inconsistent texture
- Not widely available

ZEBRA STRIPES WITH A SHOCK

With straight, alternating dark and light brown lines on quartersawn cuts, beli is easily confused with zebrawood (*Microberlinia brazzavillensis*). In fact, beli is often sold as a substitute for zebrawood, not because it is much cheaper but for its slightly better availability. The color isn't consistent and the darker lines are jagged on crown-cut sides as if they have been given a sharp electric shock. Up close the surface looks slightly pixellated, which makes it shimmer, and you may find occasional gum pockets. The best samples are used for veneer. A figured version can be found with ribbon-figure grain patterning. A very interesting wood.

KEY CHARACTERISTICS
Type Tropical hardwood
Other names *Julbernadia pellegriniana*
Sources West Africa
Color Striped light and dark brown, darkening toward the heart
Texture Medium to coarse
Grain Looks straight, but much is interlocking
Hardness Medium
Weight Heavy (50 lb./cu. ft.) (800 kg/cu. m)

AVAILABILITY AND SUSTAINABILITY

Beli is not listed as vulnerable, and is the sort of species that ought to be available from a certified source. However, it is not widely available. When you do find it, it is not expensive.

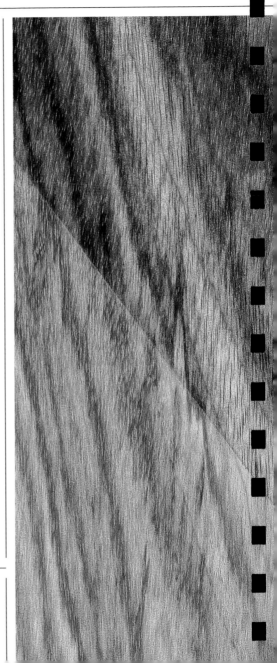

Key uses   **Interior** Furniture   **Utility** Tool handles

Decorative Veneer for paneling and cabinetmaking

Paratecoma peroba
White peroba

STRENGTHS
- Durable
- Distinctive mottled figure
- High luster

WEAKNESSES
- Unpleasant to work
- Interlocking grain

MOTTLED AND DURABLE OLIVE-COLORED HARDWOOD

This is not one of the most pleasant species to work with as it tends to be dusty, and both the dust and splinters can cause skin problems and are said to be poisonous. It is possible to achieve a beautiful smooth surface with a high luster, but the interlocking grain can be awkward to machine. Seasoning is generally easy, with only medium movement once the wood is dry, but there can be some twisting. It is naturally very durable.

KEY CHARACTERISTICS

Type Tropical hardwood
Other names Golden peroba
Sources Brazil
Color Honey to olive-brown, with darker bands and rays and some dark gum pockets
Texture Fine and even
Grain Interlocking or wavy with mottled rays across the grain on quartered sides
Hardness Hard and reasonably strong; bends reasonably well
Weight Medium to heavy (47 lb./cu. ft.) (750 kg/cu. m)

AVAILABILITY AND SUSTAINABILITY

White peroba can be found with a bit of hunting, and it is not listed as endangered. It is likely to be medium priced for a hardwood.

Key uses

Interior
Flooring
Cabinetmaking

Decorative
Veneer
Turning

Marine
Marine construction

Exterior
Decking

Joinery
Paneling

Peltogyne *species*
Purpleheart

STRENGTHS	WEAKNESSES
• Dramatic purple color	• Difficult to use
• Strong and hard	• Not widely available
• Heavy	• Interlocking grain
	• Tends to check and split

DRAMATIC HARDWOOD THAT IS PURPLE TO THE CORE

Various species of the genus *Peltogyne* are known as purpleheart, the main ones being *P. pubescens*, *P. porphyrocardia* and *P. venosa*, but one thing is clear: the lumber is purple. It is even-grained, with a moderate texture, and there is little distinction between quartersawn and slab-sawn sides. The color is largely consistent, though there can be slightly darker bands, and the wood turns dark brown with age.

KEY CHARACTERISTICS
Type Tropical hardwood
Species *P. pubescens*, *P. porphyrocardia*, *P. venosa*, *P. confertiflora*, *P. paniculata*, *P. purpurea*
Alternatives Jarrah (*Eucalyptus marginata*), African padauk (*Pterocarpus soyauxii*)
Sources Tropical South and Central America
Color Purple
Texture Moderate
Grain Varies from straight through wavy to interlocking

Hardness Hard
Weight Heavy (58 lb./cu. ft.) (930 kg/cu. m)
Strength Good, though not easy to bend
Seasoning and stability Fairly stable during and after seasoning, though it tends to be slow to dry and can split and check.
Wastage Moderate, but watch out for checks and splits.
Range of board widths Likely to be limited
Range of board thicknesses Likely to be limited
Durability Very good

IN THE WORKSHOP

Purpleheart can exude gum, which clogs cutters and blades. The gum deposits and hard wood can easily dull an edge. Go slowly and watch out for tearing where the grain is interlocked.

Milling Dulling of edges is the greatest problem.
Shaping Hard but moderately coarse, so it will take a reasonable edge and profile.
Assembly Nail and screw holes need pre-drilling, but it glues well.
Finishing Experiment on scrap before applying a finish to purpleheart, as some polishes can diminish the color. Reasonable luster.

VARIATIONS

A dye can be extracted from purpleheart for coloring textile fabrics. The lumber is fairly uniform.

SUSTAINABILITY

Purpleheart has not been reported as a threatened species, but it is advisable to check the latest listings. Some certified lumber is available, but not widely.

AVAILABILITY AND COST

Not easy to find, and can vary greatly in cost from moderate to expensive.

Key uses

Interior	Utility
Flooring	Handles

Decorative	Luxury & leisure
Turning	Billiard tables and
Veneer for paneling	cues
and cabinetmaking	

Pericopsis elata
Afrormosia

STRENGTHS
- Excellent substitute for teak
- Fine, even texture
- Subtle coloring

WEAKNESSES
- Endangered

TEAK SUBSTITUTE THAT IS ITSELF NOW RARE

There is no clearer sign of the unsustainable nature of much timber exploitation than the reduction of a species that was once considered only an alternative to finer woods. Afrormosia, from West Africa, has many of the qualities of teak (*Tectona grandis*) and has been used for years as a substitute for that Southeast Asian classic. It has similar grain, color, texture and durability, but has been listed as endangered for some years, and international trade is now restricted.

KEY CHARACTERISTICS

Type Tropical hardwood
Other names *Afrormosia elata*, African satinwood, African teak
Alternatives Teak (*Tectona grandis*)
Sources West Africa
Color Medium brown, which can be yellow or orange when freshly cut, but darkens quickly. There is a risk of blue staining.
Texture Fine and even

Grain Straight, but with some interlocking grain
Hardness Hard
Weight Medium to heavy (43 lb./cu. ft.) (690 kg/cu. m)
Strength Good
Seasoning and stability Needs to be seasoned slowly, but very stable
Wastage Low
Range of board widths Good
Range of board thicknesses Good
Durability Excellent, but can corrode ferrous metals

IN THE WORKSHOP

Not as oily as teak, afrormosia is more suitable for furniture making as it finishes well and, for a tropical hardwood, it is relatively easy to use.

Milling There is some risk of tearing, but the lumber does not tend to chip.
Shaping There will be some interlocking grain, but generally afrormosia is easy to work.
Assembly Screws and nails may need pre-drilling, as afrormosia can split, but it glues better than teak.
Finishing Good; high luster

SUSTAINABILITY

Afrormosia has been placed on the CITES Appendix I, meaning that it is at risk of extinction. There is no evidence of certified lumber.

AVAILABILITY AND COST

You can still buy afrormosia, but not with any ease. It is reasonably expensive, but not excessively so. You may find some recycled lumber, but otherwise this species is best avoided.

Key uses

Interior
Furniture
Flooring

Marine
Boat building

Joinery
Interior trim
General joinery

Picea sitchensis
Sitka spruce

STRENGTHS
- Straight grain
- Good strength-to-weight ratio
- Very easy to use

WEAKNESSES
- Needs preservative for outdoor use

RESONANT AND STRONG SOFTWOOD

Used for many purposes and confused with many other softwoods, Sitka spruce is renowned for being resonant and as a result is often used to make guitars and other musical instruments. It is particularly straight-grained and strong for its weight. The long fibers have made it popular in the manufacture of plywood for making aircraft and for pulping to make paper.

KEY CHARACTERISTICS

Type Temperate softwood
Other names Silver spruce, tideland spruce, Menzies spruce, coast spruce, yellow spruce
Related species Red spruce (*P. rubens*), black spruce (*P. mariana*), Englemann spruce (*P. engelmannii*), western white spruce (*P. glauca*)
Sources Northwest coast of United States and west coast of Canada
Color Pale straw, with pinkish hue to heartwood
Texture Uniformly medium, with coarser texture when grown faster
Grain Straight
Hardness Medium; strong for its weight and easy to bend
Weight Light (26 lb./cu. ft.) (420 kg/cu. m)

AVAILABILITY AND SUSTAINABILITY

Sitka spruce is readily available. There is no evidence that it is under threat and it is a fast-growing tree, though there is bound to be increasing pressure on old-growth trees whose high-quality wood is favored for musical instruments. Certified supplies are available. Top-quality lumber is expensive for a softwood, but not by the standards of rare exotic hardwoods.

Key uses **Luxury & leisure**
Musical instruments

Technical
Ladders
Propellers

 Joinery
Plywood

Marine
Oars
Masts

Pinus monticola
Western white pine

STRENGTHS
- Seasons well, and stable
- Fine, even texture
- Easy to work

WEAKNESSES
- Not durable

RELIABLE PINE FOR INTERIOR USE

Easily confused with white pine (*P. strobus*), western white pine is versatile and moves very little once dry, which is a key quality for a softwood. It works well, especially because the growth rings are not pronounced and the texture is fine and even, but it is not durable. As a result it is a popular choice for interior joinery, as well as for plywood. It is even used for patternmaking because the texture is easy to carve but takes a good edge. You may notice thin, darker resin lines, but they do not present problems.

KEY CHARACTERISTICS

Type Temperate softwood
Other names Idaho white pine
Related species Lodgepole or contorta pine (*P. contorta*)
Sources Western United States and Canada
Color Pale yellow; latewood is only slightly darker than earlywood
Texture Fine and even
Grain Straight
Hardness Harder than white pine (*P. strobus*), but not good for bending
Weight Light (26 lb./cu. ft.) (420 kg/cu. m)

AVAILABILITY AND SUSTAINABILITY

Widely available and not expensive. Certified supplies are obtainable.

Key uses   ▛   **Joinery**
Interior trim
Plywood

   Decorative
Patternmaking

Pinus palustris
Longleaf pine

STRENGTHS
- Distinctive grain pattern
- Good seasoning and stability

WEAKNESSES
- Contrasting density of growth rings
- Grain can make it tricky to work

STRIPY SOFTWOOD THAT IS SOFT AND HARD

The most distinctive feature of the group of species that longleaf pine belongs to (others listed below) is also the cause of their most significant weakness. The contrast between the pale earlywood and the darker, orange-red latewood can make planing by hand or machine challenging. It is grown across the southern United States and is generally used for utility purposes because it is relatively strong and has a high resin content.

KEY CHARACTERISTICS

Type Temperate softwood
Other names Southern yellow pine, yellow pine, longleaf yellow pine, Georgia pine
Similar species *P. elliottii*, shortleaf pine (*P. echinata*), loblolly pine (*P. taeda*), Caribbean pitch pine (*P. caribaea* and *P. oocarpa*)
Alternatives Douglas fir (*Pseudotsuga menziesii*)
Sources Southern United States
Color Pale yellow-cream earlywood and darker reddish orange latewood
Texture Medium
Grain Straight
Hardness Moderate

Weight Medium to heavy (42 lb./cu. ft.) (670 kg/cu. m)
Strength Good, but not for bending, as the resin protects the fibers from the softening effects of steam
Seasoning and stability Easy to season quickly, with little movement once dry
Wastage Low; few knots to worry about
Range of board widths Good
Range of board thicknesses Good
Durability Moderately resistant to decay, but prone to insect attack

IN THE WORKSHOP

Longleaf pine is not the best pine species for furniture making, notably because of its resin content and the contrast between the growth rings. This does make it an interesting choice for panels, which can look superb, with dramatic patterning.

Milling Surfaces well, though hand planes can stutter as they cross the lines of grain.
Shaping Takes a good edge, but the resin can build up on blades and cutters, reducing the effectiveness of the cut. Clean blade edges with a solvent.
Assembly Good. Glues well, and nails and screws do not need pre-drilling.
Finishing Has a good luster, but stains only moderately well because of the contrasting density of the grain. Make sure you experiment first.

VARIATIONS

Quartersawn sides have parallel lines, with flame shapes on the plain-sawn faces.

SUSTAINABILITY

No problems with sustainability. Certified supplies are readily available.

AVAILABILITY AND COST

Widely available and not expensive.

Key uses

↗ **Construction**
General construction

⌐ **Joinery**
General joinery
Exterior trim

Interior
Flooring

Exterior
Decking

Utility
Utility purposes

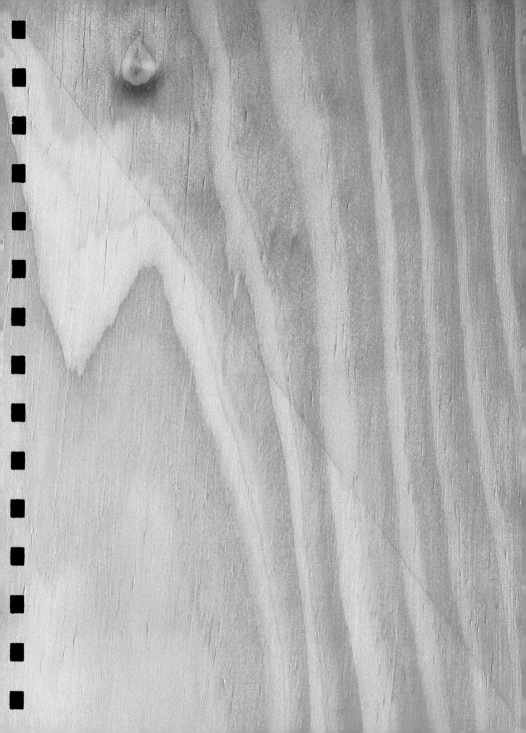

Pinus strobus
White pine

STRENGTHS
- Easy to work
- Seasons well, and stable once dry
- Uniform texture

WEAKNESSES
- Weak
- Not durable

SOFTER PINE THAT IS EASY TO WORK

A versatile lumber, also known as yellow pine, white pine is neither strong nor durable, but is easy to use for joinery and interior trim. The tree, which is fairly large for a pine, is grown down the length of North America from Canada to Mexico. Tea brewed from the leaves was once drunk at sea to ward off scurvy. Masts too were often fabricated from white pine.

KEY CHARACTERISTICS
Type Temperate softwood
Other names Eastern, western and northern white pine, yellow pine (U.K.)
Related species Jack pine (*P. banksiana*), shore pine (*P. contorta*), Canadian red pine or Norway pine (*P. resinosa*)
Alternatives Western hemlock (*Tsuga heterophylla*)
Sources North America
Color Beige to pale red-brown, with some short, fine darker lines that look like resin ducts but are not
Texture Even texture, with no great contrast between earlywood and latewood
Grain Straight
Hardness Soft

Weight Light (24 lb./cu. ft.) (380 kg/cu. m)
Strength Not strong and not recommended for bending
Seasoning and stability Very stable once dry, and easy to season, being quick to dry and shrinking very little, but it must be stacked well or there is a risk of blue staining.
Wastage Low
Range of board widths Good
Range of board thicknesses Good
Durability Poor

IN THE WORKSHOP
Many pines are more difficult to use than might be expected because of the contrast in density of the earlywood and latewood. This often makes the wood awkward to plane, with the edge jumping across the growth rings. White pine does not suffer from this problem; indeed the texture is particularly uniform, with inconspicuous growth rings.

Milling Easy to surface, with little risk of tearing.
Shaping Generally good. White pine is often used in patternmaking, which shows that it can be worked precisely.
Assembly Fine, but the lumber is very soft, so watch out for bruising, even when sanding on the bench. It screws, glues and nails very well.
Finishing Finishes better than many pines because the stain or polish is evenly distributed, is not rejected by the growth rings and does not raise the grain too badly.

VARIATIONS
Low-quality white pine is used in construction and for packing crates and pallets.

SUSTAINABILITY
Grown extensively, and under no threat.

AVAILABILITY AND COST
Widely available and economical.

Key uses

Joinery General joinery / Interior trim / Plywood

Interior Furniture

Decorative Patternmaking / Carving

Luxury & leisure Musical instruments

Marine Boat building

Prunus avium
Sweet cherry

STRENGTHS
- Distinctive grain pattern
- Subtle color

WEAKNESSES
- Poor availability
- Poor seasoning and moderate stability

SUBTLE FRUITWOOD FROM THE GARDEN

While black cherry (*P. serotina*) has won universal appeal as a contemporary mahogany substitute, sweet cherry remains a bit-player in the lumber world, and is more likely to be grown in the garden than a forest. Though it offers interesting grain patterns and color, it is not used much and availability is limited, perhaps because the trees rarely grow very large and boards are prone to warping and distortion. It does, however, share the smoothness and consistency of other fruitwoods and is ideal as a decorative feature or panel, or for turning.

KEY CHARACTERISTICS

Type Temperate hardwood
Other names *Cerasus avium*, fruit cherry, kirsche, merisier, kers, bird cherry, gean, mazzard, European cherry
Related species European bird cherry (*P. padus*)
Sources Europe and parts of Asia and North Africa
Color Light brown or tan, with some pinkish hue
Texture Even and fine
Grain Largely close-grained and straight, though with some thin latewood lines
Hardness Medium
Weight Medium (38 lb./cu. ft.) (610 kg/cu. m)

AVAILABILITY AND SUSTAINABILITY

This cherry grows extensively across Europe, and there is no threat to its future. The tree does not live very long, and lumber is likely to come from dying trees. It is not widely available.

Key uses **Decorative** Turning Veneer for paneling **Interior** Chairmaking

Prunus domestica
Plum

STRENGTHS
- Smooth, even texture
- Substitute for cherry

WEAKNESSES
- Available only in small sizes
- High wastage
- Poor stability

FRUITWOOD WITH A SMALL DIAMETER

Fruitwoods can be exquisite, with a fine, smooth and even texture and a subtle grain pattern. Plum is one of the nicest; it is very similar to black cherry, but perhaps with more color. However, it is generally sold only in limited widths because the tree never grows very large, as the trunk doesn't grow very thick. This causes stability problems, and plum is used mainly for turning.

KEY CHARACTERISTICS

Type Temperate hardwood
Other names European plum, common plum
Sources Europe, North America
Color Creamy yellow sapwood and darker mid-brown heartwood with a hint of red or pink
Texture Fine and even
Grain Straight, with a subtle pattern and little contrast in density and workability between early and latewood rings
Hardness Medium
Weight Medium to heavy (45 lb./cu. ft.) (720 kg/cu. m)

AVAILABILITY AND SUSTAINABILITY

The plum tree never grows very large nor lives that long, so supplies are likely to be limited. However, more will grow and it is not at risk. Sourcing plum may be more challenging, but it is not particularly expensive. The best place to buy plum is probably an orchard.

Key uses

Interior Chairmaking

Utility Handles

Decorative Turning

Prunus serotina
Black cherry

STRENGTHS
- Fine, even texture
- Straight grain
- Easy to use
- Finishes well

WEAKNESSES
- Lack of distinctive pattern
- Becoming expensive

LUMBER FOR THE 21ST CENTURY
Black cherry has grown in popularity recently, largely because of its combination of fine texture, wavy but even grain and mid-tone color. It has many of the qualities and feel of the best mahogany (*Swietenia* species), which is now very difficult to buy. Black cherry tends to have some dirty patches or flecks, but the wood darkens very quickly after milling and finishing to camouflage those imperfections. In fact, it is so reactive to light that you can temporarily "write" messages on a black cherry board by using a mask or stencil.

KEY CHARACTERISTICS
Type Temperate hardwood
Other names Cabinet cherry, New England mahogany, American cherry, rum cherry
Alternatives Peroba rosa (*Aspidosperma polyneuron*), European cherry (*P. avium*)
Sources North America
    Color Medium reddish brown that darkens quickly
        Texture Fine, close and even

Grain Straight
Hardness Moderately hard
Weight Medium (36 lb./cu. ft.) (580 kg/cu. m)
Strength Good
Seasoning and stability Fast-drying, without much distortion and with continued moderate movement
Wastage Low
Range of board widths Good
Range of board thicknesses Good
Durability Moderate

IN THE WORKSHOP
Black cherry is now one of the most favored lumbers in the workshop, largely because of its straight grain and fine, even texture. The figure is rarely outstanding, but the color and feel make up for that.

Milling Easy; doesn't dull blades and tends not to tear.
Shaping Profiles and joints can be cut with ease.
Assembly Good; glues, screws and nails well, and moves only moderately once dry.
Finishing Comes up to a superb luster, and takes stain well for imitating mahogany.

VARIATIONS
Though you can find a little lacewood-like figure where boards are quartersawn, the grain pattern is uniform and less interesting than in many other woods.

SUSTAINABILITY
There shouldn't be a problem with the sustainability of black cherry. Certified boards are readily available.

AVAILABILITY AND COST
Widely available, but rising in price.

Key uses

 Interior Furniture and cabinetmaking

 Joinery Quality joinery and trim

 Decorative Turning Carving

Luxury & leisure Musical instruments

Marine Boat building

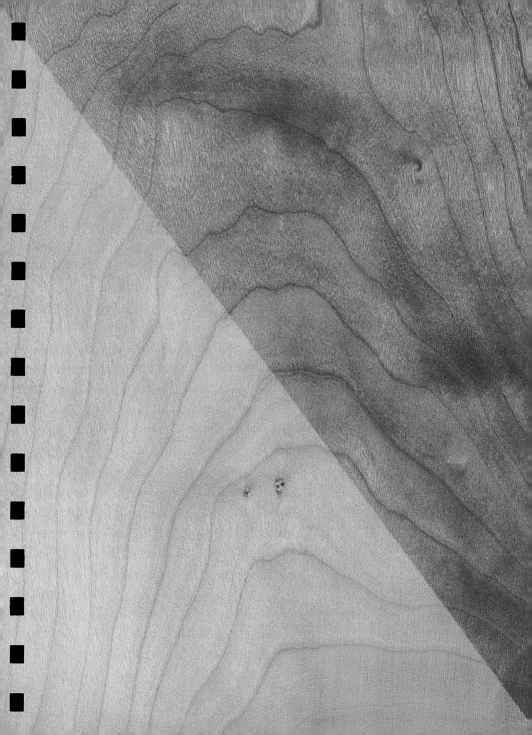

Pseudotsuga menziesii
Douglas fir

STRENGTHS
- Uniform texture
- Distinctive patterning
- Relatively strong

WEAKNESSES
- Can be brittle and splinter
- Knots can be a problem

TALL TREE WITH DISTINCTIVE GRAIN

Famous in Europe for being one of the largest trees, Douglas fir is valued for its straight grain and stability. It is distinguished by tight rings, quite similar to those of western red cedar, but paler in color and not as fibrous. Of course it is not really a fir (*Abies* genus), and its name derives from its similarities to hemlock (*Tsuga* genus). The growth rings are particularly conspicuous, producing attractive wavy lines, but the grain does not present as many problems as you might expect.

KEY CHARACTERISTICS

Type Temperate softwood
Other names Oregon pine
Alternatives Western red cedar (*Thuja plicata*)
Sources Grows from British Columbia down the western coast of the United States to Mexico
Color Pale yellowy beige contrasting with brighter reddish orange latewood lines
Texture Neither fine nor coarse, but uniform and relatively easy to work
Grain Straight, with some wavy grain
Hardness Harder than might be expected for its weight

Weight Medium (33 lb./cu. ft.) (530 kg/cu. m)
Strength Surprisingly strong, especially lumber from the Pacific coast regions.
Seasoning and stability Good; Douglas fir can be dried quickly and there is little movement once it is dry.
Wastage Medium; there may be some loose knots, but not much sapwood.
Range of board widths Good
Range of board thicknesses Good
Durability Moderate

IN THE WORKSHOP

Douglas fir is a satisfying lumber to work, with spectacular grain patterns emerging on plain-sawn surfaces, but it has its drawbacks. Cutters have to be sharp and there is a risk of splintering.

Milling Little tearing, but edges must be sharp.
Shaping Takes a good edge.
Assembly You will probably need to pre-drill for nails, as Douglas fir has a tendency to split.
Finishing Good

VARIATIONS

Quartersawn sides have very tight growth rings, with some speckling from what look like resin ducts.

SUSTAINABILITY

Not listed as in any danger, but certified supplies are available.

AVAILABILITY AND COST

Easy to buy, at moderate cost.

Key uses   **Construction** General construction   **Joinery** General joinery Plywood

Decorative Veneer   **Marine** General marine

Pterocarpus soyauxii
African padauk

STRENGTHS
- Distinctive color
- Good grain pattern
- Relatively easy to use
- Strong

WEAKNESSES
- Some interlocking grain
- Doubts regarding sustainability

HARD, STRONG AND DISTINCTIVELY RED
African padauk is sometimes known as barwood, presumably because it is moisture-resistant and can survive knocks. The moderately coarse texture is consistent, though the deep red color is streaked with darker lines. It is liked by woodworkers because it is tough but relatively easy to use, even though the grain can be interlocking in patches, otherwise being straight or wavy. It is often used for flooring because it wears very slowly.

KEY CHARACTERISTICS
Type Tropical hardwood
Other names Barwood, African coralwood
Related species Burma padauk (*P. macrocarpus*), narra (*P. indicus*), Andaman padauk (*P. dalbergioides*)
Alternatives Jarrah (*Eucalyptus marginata*)
Sources Central and West Africa
Color Red, which darkens to purple-brown quickly
Texture Moderately coarse, but consistent
Grain Straight, but slightly wavy, with some interlocking

Hardness Very tough
Weight Medium to heavy (c .45 lb./cu. ft.) (720 kg/cu. m)
Strength Moderate to good
Seasoning and stability Excellent on both counts
Wastage Low
Range of board widths Reasonable
Range of board thicknesses Reasonable
Durability Good

IN THE WORKSHOP
African padauk is much easier and more satisfying to use than you might expect of a lumber that appears to have a coarse, interlocking grain. Because of this it is highly prized and exploited, and many species of padauk have been listed as vulnerable.

Milling Good, with little blunting.
Shaping Being hard and only moderately coarse it can be shaped easily, and joint cutting is good.
Assembly Good; takes screws, nails and glue well.
Finishing Excellent; high luster and superb color.

VARIATIONS
African padauk has the sort of consistent figure that does not generate remarkable effects from different cuts, though decorative results can be achieved by quarter-sawing Burma padauk.

SUSTAINABILITY
Woodworkers should exercise some caution when using padauk, though African padauk does not appear to have been listed as vulnerable. Other species, particularly Andaman padauk, are much rarer. Very little certified padauk is available.

AVAILABILITY AND COST
May be difficult to find, and is likely to be expensive.

Key uses

Interior
Furniture
Work surfaces
Flooring

Decorative
Veneer for paneling and cabinetmaking
Turning

Pyrus communis
Common pear

STRENGTHS
- Fine, even and creamy texture
- Subtle coloring
- Stable and strong

WEAKNESSES
- Not widely available
- Limited supply

THE TRUE CHAMPION OF FRUITWOODS

Though black cherry (*Prunus serotina*) is now ubiquitous, pear is one of the most prized of the fruitwoods, coming up a pale pink-brown, with a fine, even texture and gentle wavy grain. Like other fruitwoods it has a creamy feel, and is favored by chairmakers and the manufacturers of musical and measuring instruments. Stained black, it is often used as a substitute for ebony, and has many of the same qualities. It is often used for marquetry. Pear is not usually available in wide boards, and is often attacked by pests, but it is very stable. The best lumber is said to come from France and Germany.

KEY CHARACTERISTICS
Type Temperate hardwood
Other names European pear (U.S.), pearwood (U.K.)
Alternatives Peroba rosa (*Aspidosperma polyneuron*), black cherry (*Prunus serotina*)
Sources Europe and North America
Color Pale brown, with a pink hue
Texture Fine and even
Grain Wavy, but not interlocking

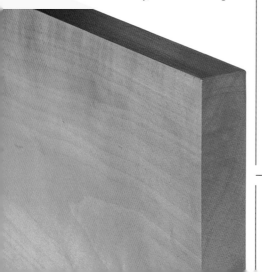

Hardness Medium
Weight Medium to heavy (44 lb./cu. ft.) (700 kg/cu. m)
Strength Surprisingly strong
Seasoning and stability Seasons slowly and tends to distort and warp. But once dry it is very stable.
Wastage Distortion may affect boards, but there is little contrast between sapwood and heartwood. Wastage should be moderate, but will be high if you are converting your own branches or trunks. If you choose to do this, kiln-dry the lumber.
Range of board widths Poor
Range of board thicknesses Likely to be very limited
Durability Not particularly good, but both heartwood and sapwood can be protected with preservative.

IN THE WORKSHOP

Like most fruitwoods, pear is relatively easy to work, being even in texture. It is particularly popular for turning.

Milling Causes moderate dulling, but otherwise it machines well.
Shaping Turns very well, and will take a good edge or profile.
Assembly Fine; glues, screws and nails well.
Finishing Polishes easily to a beautiful luster with any finish.

VARIATIONS

Common pear is often steamed for a richer color. The quartersawn cuts can reveal a mottled figure.

SUSTAINABILITY

It is very difficult to evaluate the status of pear. As it is a fruit-bearing tree more will always be planted, and only old trees that are large enough will be felled. These will probably have ceased bearing fruit, and will hopefully be replaced after felling.

AVAILABILITY AND COST

Common pear has limited availability, especially the best European lumber, and is likely to be quite expensive.

Key uses		**Decorative** Veneer for marquetry and bandings Turning Carving		**Interior** Furniture making
				Luxury & leisure Musical instruments
				Technical Measuring instruments

Quercus alba
White oak

STRENGTHS
- Straight grain
- Low wastage
- Few defects
- Good value
- Widely available
- Certified lumber available

WEAKNESSES
- Can lack character

STURDY HARDWOOD THAT IS CLEAN AND STRAIGHT

White oak is hard to fault. It is easy to use, good value for a temperate hardwood, versatile and widely available from certified sources. The straight grain and consistent texture suit many modern styles, and are valuable in batch production. The wood's one real weakness is its lack of distinctive figure and absence of the defects that some woodworkers favor for character.

KEY CHARACTERISTICS
Type Temperate hardwood
Other names American white oak (U.K.)
Alternatives Japanese oak (*Q. mongolica*), red oak (*Q. rubra*)
Sources Canada and United States
Color Beige to medium brown, which finishes as a rich honey color
Texture Medium to coarse
Grain Usually straight
Hardness Hard

Weight Medium to heavy (48 lb./cu. ft.) (770 kg/cu. m)
Strength Strong, and with straight grain it bends well.
Seasoning and stability Cracks and checks may appear if it is dried too quickly. Moves moderately once used.
Wastage Low; clean and straight-grained
Range of board widths Good
Range of board thicknesses Good
Durability Fine for external use, but the heartwood will not take preservatives for better protection.

IN THE WORKSHOP
White oak can be planed and cut effortlessly, exuding the typical oak smell but without any of the changing grain patterns of English oak (*Q. robur*). Panels can be constructed with ease, as the consistent figure hides the joins. The only problem might be the slight variation in color across a board, from pale to darker brown. Wood from slower-grown trees is likely to be easier to use, with a more even texture and narrower rings.

Milling Easy
Shaping Routing a profile is very simple, though it can chip a little, and cutting joints is easy.
Assembly Some woodworkers may tell you the gluing needs care, but we have never had any problems.
Finishing Takes most finishes beautifully, and sands to a fine surface. The open grain is ideal for liming paste, but stain doesn't always take evenly.

VARIATIONS
Used for decorative veneering and book matching.

SUSTAINABILITY
There is plenty of certified white oak. Where it is grown on a plantation the only issue might be one of biodiversity within the forests, but certification covers that aspect as well. No threat of extinction.

AVAILABILITY AND COST
Widely available and relatively inexpensive, with a low wastage rate.

Key uses		
Interior Furniture Cabinetmaking Flooring	**Construction** General construction	**Joinery** Internal joinery Store interiors

Quercus robur
English oak

STRENGTHS
- Distinctive color and grain pattern
- Strong and firm, but relatively easy to use
- Open texture can be used for special effects

WEAKNESSES
- Can be expensive
- High wastage because of defects and shakes
- Wavy grain can be difficult to work

THE CLASSIC HARDWOOD

English oak is renowned for its coarse grain, distinctive medullary rays and wavy grain. Quartersawn lumber is used for the finest woodwork, being stable and strong, while slab-cut wood has wild flames of grain and is used in all forms of decorative woodwork. Popular with turners for its color, grain and coarse texture, English oak is still widely used for traditional house building, especially when green and unseasoned.

KEY CHARACTERISTICS

Type Temperate hardwood
Other names European oak, truffle oak
Alternatives White oak (*Q. alba*), red oak (*Q. rubra*)
Sources Europe
Color Light brown, with a golden hue
Texture Coarse. Soft tissue can be worn away with a wire brush or by sandblasting for special effects.
Grain Can be very wavy
Weight Medium to heavy (45–47 lb./ cu. ft.) (720–750 kg/cu. m)
Hardness Hard

Strength High
Seasoning and stability Usually air-dried, slowly. There is a great risk of checking and splitting, which adds to wastage.
Wastage Often high, with wide sapwood and waney edges
Range of board widths Good, with wide boards available
Range of board thicknesses Good
Durability Excellent; oak was used to make early battleships.

IN THE WORKSHOP

You either love or hate working with English oak. You can be caught out by the wavy grain that seems to chip whichever way you work.

Milling Wavy grain means that it can chip easily, and milling requires sharp blades and fine cuts. Some oak can be abrasive and can dull edges.
Shaping Takes an edge beautifully for molding and paneling, but will chip.
Assembly Glues well, and tight joints are relatively easy to cut. Water-based adhesives can tarnish the surface if in contact with steel clamps. Acid in the oak causes steel screws or nails to corrode, so use brass or alloy fittings.
Finishing Beautiful and easy to finish with oil, wax, shellac polishes, polyurethane or lacquers. Coarse-grain wood is rarely filled, but English oak stains well for color or just to darken it a little.

VARIATIONS

Quartersawn oak is traditionally used for drawer linings. Burl oak is popular with turners and as veneer for furniture and cabinet work. The diseased heart of some dying oaks is dark, and is known as brown oak.

SUSTAINABILITY

There is a growing quantity of English oak from certified sustainable sources, but it is generally safe to use.

AVAILABILITY AND COST

Good English oak can be expensive and wastage rates can be high.

Key uses			
	Interior Cabinet and furniture making Flooring		**Joinery** Interior joinery
	Construction Traditional house construction		**Decorative** Turning
			Marine Boat building

Quercus rubra
Red oak

STRENGTHS
- Economical and abundant
- Reddish brown color

WEAKNESSES
- Less figure than other oaks
- Difficult to season

ECONOMICAL OAK WITH LESS FIGURE

Red oak lacks the patterning or figuring of rays that is found in white oak (*Q. alba*) or English oak (*Q. robur*), but it has deeper color. It is generally cheaper than white oak and less popular with woodworkers. However, it should not be discounted, especially lumber that is grown farther north, where the slower growth produces more consistent color and grain. Watch out for sapwood, which should be avoided with oak and is not always counted as a defect.

KEY CHARACTERISTICS

Type Temperate hardwood
Other names Northern red oak, southern red oak
Related species *Q. falcata*
Alternatives English oak (*Q. robur*)
Sources North America
Color Reddish brown
Texture Medium to coarse
Grain Straight
  Hardness Hard
    Weight Medium to heavy (48 lb./cu. ft.)
      (770 kg/cu. m)

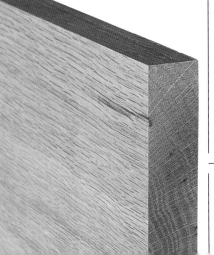

Strength Medium, and bends well
Seasoning and stability Best seasoned slowly, but there is always a risk of checking, splits and honeycombing. Moderately stable once seasoned.
Wastage Moderate, because of defects that result from seasoning
Range of board widths Good
Range of board thicknesses Good
Durability Poor; prone to rot and insect attack

IN THE WORKSHOP

Many oaks are infamous for dulling tool edges, and red oak is no exception. Most woodworkers love the unique smell of oak in their workshop.

Milling Planes well, but there is always a risk of chipping where the grain curves toward the edge.
Shaping Easy to cut and takes a superb edge.
Assembly The critical thing to remember with oak is that it reacts badly with ferrous metals. Steel screws will corrode and eventually break, while also staining the wood. Water-based glues can stain the wood if in contact with ferrous clamps.
Finishing Finishes well with any application and is especially good for liming and staining.

VARIATIONS

Quartersawn sides have some ray figure, but it is neither as extensive nor as pronounced as in other oaks.

SUSTAINABILITY

Abundant and in no danger, and certified supplies are relatively easy to find.

AVAILABILITY AND COST

Widely available, and more economical than white oak.

Key uses

Interior
Furniture and cabinetmaking
Flooring

Joinery
Interior trim
General joinery

Sequoia sempervirens
Redwood

STRENGTHS
- Durable outside
- Easy to work
- Lightweight

WEAKNESSES
- Tendency to split or splinter
- Not durable underground

STRAIGHT-GRAINED SOFTWOOD FOR EXTERIOR USE

Redwood is distinguished by its deep color and by a very straight grain, with close-spaced growth rings that give it a fibrous look and feel. It is not strong and has a tendency to split, but that makes it ideal for splitting into shingles. Redwood is also durable, as long as it is not in contact with the ground, and is used extensively for exterior joinery, roofing, decking and cladding. Watch out for splintering when working the lumber by hand or machine, and check that adhesives will not stain the wood.

KEY CHARACTERISTICS

Type Temperate softwood
Other names Californian redwood, sequoia, coast redwood, Humboldt redwood
Related species Wellingtonia (*Sequoiadendron giganteum*), giant redwood (*S. gigantea*)
Sources Pacific coast of the United States
Color Dark reddish brown, with close growth rings but low luster
Texture Generally uniform and fine, but can be coarse
Grain Straight
Hardness Soft
Weight Light (26 lb./cu. ft.) (420 kg/cu. m)

AVAILABILITY AND SUSTAINABILITY

The supply of redwood is now restricted and prices have risen to make it expensive for a softwood. Certified supplies are available.

Key uses

Joinery
Exterior joinery

 Exterior
Fences
Greenhouses
Garden furniture
Decking

Construction
Roofing
Cladding

 Interior
Flooring

Sickingia salvadorensis
Chakte kok

STRENGTHS
- Dramatic patterning
- Good luster

WEAKNESSES
- Limited dimensions
- Risk of splits and defects

DRAMATIC RED WOOD WITH STRIPES

Chakte kok, which is spelled in many ways, displays marvelous grain patterns, with wavy lines of dark brown and bright pink-red. The swirling end-grain indicates interlocking grain that needs sharp tools to work. The contrasting sapwood ages to a pale yellow. Reportedly durable, the lumber surfaces and turns well and is generally fairly easy to work. It polishes to a good luster. Some of the problems woodworkers will face are inconsistent color and narrow stock, which may increase wastage, and there is some risk of checks and insect holes.

KEY CHARACTERISTICS

Type Tropical hardwood
Other names Cuban mahogany, aguano, cobano
Sources Central America, Mexico
Color Bright red and pink, with darker meandering lines
Texture Fine and uniform
Grain Straight but bound to be interlocking
Hardness Hard
Weight Medium to heavy (40 lb./cu. ft.) (640 kg/cu. m)

AVAILABILITY AND SUSTAINABILITY

Because chakte kok is a lesser-known species, it is not widely available. This means, though, that it probably has not been overexploited, and that there are therefore manageable stocks that can be certified. Chakte kok could be used instead of bloodwood (*Brosimum paraense*).

Key uses | **Interior** Furniture Flooring | **Decorative** Turning Carving

Swietenia macrophylla
American mahogany

STRENGTHS
- Classic color and grain pattern
- Stable
- Relatively inexpensive
- Widely available

WEAKNESSES
- Tendency to tear
- Inconsistent hardness
- Quite soft and easily bruised

THE NEXT BEST THING TO CUBAN MAHOGANY
Of the many woods around the world that are referred to as mahogany, *Swietenia macrophylla* is about the only true mahogany that is commercially available. Since Cuban mahogany (*S. mahogani*) is now all but extinct, American mahogany is considered the best type available. It has the pink color of Cuban mahogany, but the texture and grain pattern is less consistent.

KEY CHARACTERISTICS
Type Tropical hardwood
Other names Honduras mahogany, Brazilian mahogany, big leaf mahogany, true mahogany
Similar species Venezuelan mahogany (*S. candollei*)
Alternatives Black cherry (*Prunus serotina*), pearwood (*Pyrus communis*), Cuban mahogany (*S. mahogani*)
Sources Central and South America
Color Varying streaks of pink to red, to dark red and brown
Texture Medium to coarse, and generally even, though bands can vary
Grain Mainly straight, but also interlocked

Hardness Medium, but you can hit harder streaks.
Weight Medium to heavy (40 lb./cu. ft.) (640 kg/cu. m)
Strength Poor to medium
Seasoning and stability Generally good to season, and with little movement once dry.
Wastage Low
Range of board widths Good
Range of board thicknesses Good
Durability Prone to some insect attack but durable outside.

IN THE WORKSHOP
Much more variable than Cuban mahogany, the American species can be tricky to work, because the grain is inconsistent and it can tear easily.

Milling Keep edges very sharp to avoid the risk of tearing. With care you can achieve a fine surface.
Shaping There is a risk of tearing with router cutters, so make gradual passes. American mahogany will take a good profile and joints can be cut simply and accurately.
Assembly The wood glues, screws and nails well, and there is some tolerance when it comes to clamping.
Finishing Stains and polishes well to a fine luster.

VARIATIONS
Plain-sawn boards can produce marvelous flame-figured mahogany (large U-shaped patterns of grain), which is ideal for panels. Alternatively there is crotch mahogany, which is cut from the join between the trunk and a branch, and used mainly for veneer for cabinets, doors and panels. Special effects, usually available as veneer, include fiddleback, mottle, pommelle, stripe and curl.

SUSTAINABILITY
American mahogany has been said to be vulnerable in some regions, but certified lumber is available. It is listed in CITES Appendix II.

AVAILABILITY AND COST
Good supplies of American mahogany are available. Its price competes well with black cherry and black walnut.

Key uses		Interior		Joinery
		Furniture making		Paneling
		Cabinetmaking		Quality joinery

Taxus baccata
English yew

STRENGTHS
- Superb color and grain pattern
- Fine, even texture
- Strong

WEAKNESSES
- Difficult to use
- Limited sizes
- Not widely available

EXOTIC SOFTWOOD THAT IS VERY HARD

English, or European, yew is a coniferous softwood, though the lumber is so hard and strong you would be forgiven for thinking it was a hardwood. The wood was often used for bows because it bends well. Today there is only a limited supply of wide, straight-grained yew. Narrower branches and roundwood are favored by turners.

KEY CHARACTERISTICS

Type Temperate softwood
Similar species Pacific or Western yew (*T. brevifolia*)
Sources Europe, some parts of Asia and north Africa
Color Heartwood is a light orange-red brown, which darkens considerably with age. The sapwood, which some woodworkers use for contrast, is white.
Texture Fine and even
Grain Varies greatly, from straight-grained to wavy or even interlocking.
Hardness Hard
Weight Medium to heavy (42 lb./cu. ft.) (670 kg/cu. m)
Strength Bends well when straight-grained, but otherwise only moderately strong and can be brittle.

Seasoning and stability Seasons well and quickly, and is stable in use.
Wastage Can be high, as boards are often cut from small-diameter roundwood, with a high proportion of sapwood and frequent knots.
Range of board widths Very limited
Range of board thicknesses Very limited
Durability Good, but can be attacked by insects, and cannot be protected by preservative.

IN THE WORKSHOP

Many woodworkers love yew for the color and grain pattern, but recognize that it can be tricky to use because of its hardness and the risk of tearing. Turners needn't worry about this, because they cut across the grain.

Milling Needs great care and a sharp edge, as yew is hard and does have a tendency to tear where the grain changes direction. Where the grain is straight, it is a joy to work.
Shaping Being hard, yew takes a sharp profile, but is unforgiving when it comes to cutting and assembling joints. Yew can be shaped easily, and to exquisite effect.
Assembly Difficult to match strips to assemble panels unless they are straight-grained. Yew does not split easily, though it is hard enough to need pre-drilling.
Finishing You may need to use a cabinet scraper for the best finish, as yew tears so easily, but it finishes to a superb luster and takes all finishes.

VARIATIONS

Solid burl yew is very highly prized by woodturners and furniture makers, and the veneer is favored by cabinetmakers. Yew veneer tends to buckle.

SUSTAINABILITY

Certified English yew is relatively rare; the tree is more commonly found in parks, churchyards and gardens than in forests and woodlands.

AVAILABILITY AND COST

English yew is rare and often very expensive.

Key uses		
Interior	Furniture	
Decorative	Turning Veneer for cabinet-making	
Luxury & leisure	Bows Musical instruments	

Taxus brevifolia
Western yew

STRENGTHS

- Beautiful grain pattern
- Distinctive color
- Very durable
- Good for steam bending

WEAKNESSES

- Rare and expensive
- Difficult to work
- High wastage

HARD SOFTWOOD WITH MEDICINAL QUALITIES

Though the berries of yew have traditionally been considered poisonous, the anticancer drug Taxol is extracted from yew. The tree is very slow growing, while the lumber is hard and good for bending, and often used in the making of archery bows. The leaves are slightly shorter than those of English yew trees (*T. baccata*), hence the Latin name *T. brevifolia*.

KEY CHARACTERISTICS

Type Temperate softwood
Other names Oregon yew, Pacific yew
Similar species English yew (*T. baccata*)
Alternatives Red maple (*Acer rubrum*)
Sources West coast of North America, from Alaska to California
Color Orange brown, which dulls and darkens with age
Texture Very fine and even
Grain Straighter than English yew, but still wavy and interlocking at times
Hardness Hard
Weight Medium to heavy
(46 lb./cu. ft.)
(740 kg/cu. m)

Strength Strong and good for bending
Seasoning and stability Stable once seasoned, but prone to shakes during the slow drying process.
Wastage Moderate to high due to defects and bands of contrasting white sapwood
Range of board widths Reasonable
Range of board thicknesses Reasonable
Durability Very good with respect to both insect attack and moisture

IN THE WORKSHOP

Though it turns and bends very well, yew can be tricky to work if your tools are not very sharp, particularly as the grain direction can change near defects. Some people find the dust irritating.

Milling Take care when surfacing around knots, where the grain can tear.
Shaping Hard enough to take a superb edge, though knots and defects can break off an edge or profile.
Assembly Care is needed when using nails as they can split the lumber, but screws are fine and it glues well.
Finishing Finishes to a superb luster, though you may need to use a cabinet scraper where the grain is difficult. Any finish will raise the color.

VARIATIONS

Burl yew is highly prized in the solid by turners and as a veneer by cabinetmakers and coachfitters. The sapwood can be used for contrast.

SUSTAINABILITY

Yew trees are precious and should be protected. You are unlikely to find certified lumber, but yew has not been listed as vulnerable.

AVAILABILITY AND COST

Rare and expensive.

Key uses	Decorative	Luxury & leisure
	Furniture and cabinetry details	Bows
	Turning	Musical instruments
	Veneer for cabinet-making	

Tectona grandis
Teak

STRENGTHS
- Oily and durable
- Attractive grain and color

WEAKNESSES
- Rare
- Tough on tools

FAMOUSLY DURABLE MARINE CLASSIC

Darker and more oily than afrormosia (*Pericopsis elata*), teak has for centuries been the first-choice species for boat building and other marine uses, and numerous pieces of garden furniture are made from the wood. Exploitation has eventually led to the development of plantations in some Asian countries, though many imitations are used as substitutes for this most durable of species.

KEY CHARACTERISTICS

Type Tropical hardwood
Alternatives Tuart (*Eucalyptus gomphocephala*)
Sources Mainly Southeast Asia, but also some growth in the Caribbean and West Africa
Color Golden honey-brown, with darker streaks. The color darkens when exposed to light.
Texture Medium coarse, with a tendency toward unevenness
Grain Straight or wavy
Hardness Hard

Weight Medium to heavy (40 lb./cu. ft.) (640 kg/cu. m)
Strength For its weight, teak is pretty strong and it can be bent, but it can also be brittle.
Seasoning and stability Seasons slowly but well, and is stable once dry.
Wastage Low
Range of board widths Good
Range of board thicknesses Good
Durability Excellent

IN THE WORKSHOP

Teak is one of the greatest species for woodworkers of all disciplines, though not as easy to use as some of the other classic woods. It is oily to touch and relatively coarse in texture.

Milling Blades must be sharp, but teak planes nicely without too much risk of tearing or chipping.
Shaping Takes a superb edge.
Assembly The oily nature can make gluing difficult, so experiment first, but screws and nails are easy to use.
Finishing It is best to experiment with finishes because of the oiliness; otherwise teak finishes well to a reasonable luster.

VARIATIONS

Some woodworkers believe old-growth teak to be of higher quality than plantation-grown lumber.

SUSTAINABILITY

Environmentally conscious woodworkers prefer to buy either plantation teak or teak from a certified source, though it is not listed as endangered.

AVAILABILITY AND COST

Expensive and now largely available only from plantations.

Key uses

▲ **Marine**
Boat building
Marine purposes

🏠 **Interior**
Flooring

 Exterior
Garden furniture
Decking

Terminalia ivorensis
Idigbo

STRENGTHS
- Economical for a hardwood
- Durable outside
- Good luster

WEAKNESSES
- Bland
- Interlocking grain
- Difficult to work

HARD-WORKING LUMBER THAT IS ALSO HARD TO WORK

Undistinguished when it comes to color and grain, idigbo is one of many African hardwoods that are used extensively for joinery inside and out and for making plywood or mass-produced furniture. Though the grain is generally straight, the texture is coarse and can be uneven, and there is a chance of interlocking grain. There are very few knots or defects, which keeps wastage low and makes the species ideal for producing joinery and furniture by machines that can force their way through unhelpful grain. There is a risk of staining when the lumber comes in contact with iron or steel in moist conditions.

KEY CHARACTERISTICS
Type Tropical hardwood
Other names Black afara, African teak
Sources West Africa
Color Pale yellow-brown
Texture Coarse
Grain Straight, but occasionally interlocking
Hardness Medium to hard
Weight Medium (35 lb./cu. ft.) (560 kg/cu. m)

AVAILABILITY AND SUSTAINABILITY
Idigbo tends to be supplied to the joinery and furniture trades; availability for home woodworkers is more limited. Species from Africa have to be regarded with some caution, and idigbo has been listed as vulnerable, but certified supplies are rare.

Key uses **Interior**
Mass-produced furniture

Joinery
Interior and exterior joinery
Plywood

Terminalia superba
Limba

STRENGTHS
- Inexpensive
- Easy to work

WEAKNESSES
- Splinters easily
- Coarse texture
- Not durable

BLACK-AND-WHITE AFRICAN HARDWOOD

Closely related to idigbo (*T. ivorensis*), limba is most commonly available in its paler form and usually known as white limba or korina. With a fairly coarse texture and generally straight grain, it is prone to splintering, and the shards can cause skin irritation. Nails and screws must be pre-drilled to prevent splintering. However, limba works fairly well and can be finished to a good luster. It is not a particularly special lumber, being valued mainly as a utility wood, though the heartwood (often known as black limba) has dark streaks and is an inexpensive alternative to zebrawood (*Microberlinia brazzavillensis*), ziricote (*Cordia dodecandra*) or marblewood (*Marmaroxylon racemosum*).

KEY CHARACTERISTICS
Type Tropical hardwood
Other names Korina, black limba, white limba, afara
Sources West Africa
Color Pale yellow or light tan
Texture Medium to coarse, but consistent
Grain Straight, but occasionally interlocking
Hardness Medium to hard, but not durable, and susceptible to insect attack
Weight Medium (34 lb./cu. ft.) (540 kg/cu. m)

AVAILABILITY AND SUSTAINABILITY
Limba is not widely available but should not be difficult to find or expensive to buy. This is one of the less popular species to be exploited commercially and has not been listed as endangered. Certified lumber is rare.

Key uses	Construction	Joinery
	General construction	Plywood Interior trim Carpentry

Thuja plicata
Western red cedar

STRENGTHS
- Naturally durable
- Straight grain

WEAKNESSES
- Coarse texture
- Weak
- Can corrode metals

AROMATIC AND DURABLE UTILITY SOFTWOOD

The straight grain and durability of western red cedar, which is not a true cedar, make it popular for building greenhouses and sheds. Being quite weak, it might be thought unsuitable for the small sections that are needed in the production of greenhouses, but the straight grain means that it is easy to use, with limited risk of splintering. That it is lightweight helps too. The bark can be used for making rope.

KEY CHARACTERISTICS

Type Temperate softwood
Other names Giant arborvitae, canoe cedar, shinglewood, giant cedar
Similar species Sequoia or redwood (*Sequoia sempervirens*), white cedar (*T. occidentalis*)
Sources North America and Europe
Color Red-brown, but sometimes pink with contrasting white sapwood. Ages to a silver-gray color that needs no finishing for outdoor use.
Texture Coarse
Grain Straight

Hardness Soft
Weight Light (23 lb./cu. ft.) (370 kg/cu. m)
Strength Weak and does not bend well
Seasoning and stability Seasons best when milled into thin boards. Very stable once dry.
Wastage Low
Range of board widths Good
Range of board thicknesses Good
Durability Generally good

IN THE WORKSHOP

The straight grain is prized in the workshop for outdoor projects. Because it splits easily, and the thin boards season fast and well, western red cedar is favored for the making of shingles. Some woodworkers complain that the dust causes skin and breathing problems.

Milling Considering it is light and coarse, western red cedar surfaces to a good finish without tainting blades with too much resin.
Shaping Can be profiled easily for making glazing bars for greenhouses, and the straight grain tends not to tear.
Assembly Glues, nails and screws well, but tends to tear when crosscut to length, so achieving a good finish to the ends of boards can be awkward.
Finishing An advantage of the color and aged patina is that western red cedar hardly needs any finishing. It does not take preservatives well, but is naturally durable.

SUSTAINABILITY

There is some concern that the best western red cedar is running out and that the species does not regenerate readily. Certified western red cedar is available.

AVAILABILITY AND COST

The supply of good western red cedar is gradually diminishing, and therefore it is rising in price, but it is still an economical lumber for outdoor projects.

Key uses		Exterior		Marine
		Sheds and greenhouses Fencing Decking		Canoes

Tilia americana
Basswood

STRENGTHS
- Superb for carving
- Fine, even texture
- Easy to season
- Inexpensive

WEAKNESSES
- Bland yellow appearance
- Defects and knots
- Some mottled staining

CARVER'S HARDWOOD WITH FEW DISTINGUISHING FEATURES

It is fortunate for basswood that it is so well suited to woodcarving and patternmaking, as there is not much else to say for it. Its critical quality is that there is no contrast between the earlywood and latewood, which means a carving chisel can cut against the lie of the grain as well as with the grain. This is unusual in wood, as normally the latewood would tear as you attempt to work against its natural bias. Otherwise basswood, like European linden (*Tilia x europaea*), is almost featureless, and finishes to a yellow color.

KEY CHARACTERISTICS
Type Temperate hardwood
Other names *T. glabra*, whitewood, American linden
Similar species *T. nigra*, *T. latifolia*
Alternatives Jelutong (*Dyera costulata*)
Sources Eastern North America
Color Creamy white to light tan, with a pink hue; yellows when a finish is applied.
Texture Fine and even

Grain Straight; hardly any noticeable difference between latewood and earlywood
Hardness Soft
Weight Light (26 lb./cu. ft.) (420 kg/cu. m)
Strength Weak and does not bend well
Seasoning and stability Good; stable once dry
Wastage Medium. May have large knots or defects and some pale mottled staining, but this only rarely affects the kinds of uses for which basswood is famed.
Range of board widths Good
Range of board thicknesses Good. Most woodcarvers are looking for thick basswood.
Durability Poor, and prone to insect attack, especially the sapwood.

IN THE WORKSHOP

Basswood is one of the easiest woods to use, and is superb for introducing children to woodworking. Fortunately it is not expensive, so mistakes are not costly.

Milling Planes well without dulling tools.
Shaping Takes a good edge and profile for such a soft wood. Carves and turns well, and joints are very easy to cut.
Assembly Good. Glues, screws and nails well without the need for pre-drilling.
Finishing Comes up to a good luster. Stains well.

VARIATIONS

Some medullary rays show a mottled effect on quarter-sawn sides, but this is neither conspicuous nor extensive.

SUSTAINABILITY

Basswood trees grow extensively across eastern North America, so there is no particular need to use certified supplies.

AVAILABILITY AND COST

Available mainly from specialist suppliers, but not expensive.

Key uses	Decorative Carving Patternmaking	Utility General use
	Luxury & leisure Modelmaking	

Tilia x europaea
European linden

STRENGTHS
- Fine, even texture
- Can be cut in any direction
- Consistent

WEAKNESSES
- Soft
- Bland
- Yellows with age

Weight Medium (34 lb./cu. ft.) (540 kg/cu. m)
Strength Moderate; can be bent and won't split.
Seasoning and stability Will move slightly even when dry, and can split during seasoning.
Wastage Moderate; may contain some knots and splits (particularly end splits) that need to be avoided. Not much sapwood.
Range of board widths Good
Range of board thicknesses Thicker pieces, suitable for carving, are often available.
Durability Not very durable

CLASSIC WOODCARVER'S LUMBER

Linden is the lumber of choice for woodcarvers in Europe, just as basswood (*T. americana*) is in the United States, and it is not used for much else. The texture is fine and even, the grain is straight and close, and the wood cuts easily and without tearing. In other words, it is everything a carver could hope for. The only disadvantage is that the color and patterning are bland, and the wood yellows with age. There are patches of shimmering medullary rays on quartersawn faces or edges, but the lumber isn't valued for these.

IN THE WORKSHOP
With grain that is fibrous, woolly and soft, lime is much more suited to carving than working with machines.

Milling Surfaces well enough, but is soft and bruises easily.
Shaping Use thin chisels or gouges and you can work a superb edge, but you may need to reduce the cutting angle for profiling.
Assembly Fine; glues well, and does not split when nailed.
Finishing Good; stains and polishes easily.

KEY CHARACTERISTICS
Type Temperate hardwood
Other names *T. vulgaris*, European lime
Alternatives Basswood (*T. americana*), jelutong (*Dyera costulata*)
Sources Europe
Color Cream
Texture Very fine and even
Grain Close and straight
Hardness Medium-soft

SUSTAINABILITY
Fine; lime grows abundantly and quickly across Europe.

AVAILABILITY AND COST
Readily available in Europe and not too expensive. The same is true for basswood in the United States.

Key uses

Decorative Carving

Utility Handles Cutting boards

Luxury & leisure Toys

Tsuga heterophylla
Western hemlock

STRENGTHS

- Straight grain
- Consistent, even texture
- Aromatic
- Stable

WEAKNESSES

- Uninteresting pattern and color
- Soft

HARD-WORKING QUALITY SOFTWOOD

Hemlock is one of the higher-quality softwoods and is used for joinery and interior trim where a hardwood would cost more but something better than an ordinary softwood is required. It is commonly used for stair components, particularly balusters. It is not, however, durable, so it is used only indoors. Hemlock has a lovely smell and is very easy to use, and is favored for all manner of construction and joinery tasks and also for veneer.

KEY CHARACTERISTICS

Type Temperate softwood
Other names Pacific hemlock, Alaska pine, hemlock spruce, British Columbia hemlock
Related species White hemlock (*T. canadensis*), Japanese hemlock (*T. sieboldii* and *T. diversifolia*), Chinese hemlock (*T. chinensis*)
Alternatives Yellow birch (*Betula alleghaniensis*), western red cedar (*Thuja plicata*)
Sources North America and Europe

Color Light golden brown, with tight rings
Texture Fine and even
Grain Straight
Hardness Soft to medium for a softwood
Weight Medium (31 lb./cu. ft.) (500 kg/cu. m)
Strength Moderate
Seasoning and stability Stable once dry, with little movement, but can be tricky to season, especially thicker boards, which can check.
Wastage Low
Range of board widths Good
Range of board thicknesses Good
Durability Poor

IN THE WORKSHOP

Less resinous than many softwoods, hemlock is easy to use except when there are knots, which can be particularly hard to work.

Milling Surfaces well, with the straight grain reducing the risk of tearing.
Shaping Takes a good edge for profiling.
Assembly Glues, nails and screws very well.
Finishing Can be stained or polished easily. Has a good luster.

SUSTAINABILITY

No obvious reason for concern, though hemlock is available from certified sources.

AVAILABILITY AND COST

Widely available and not expensive.

Key uses ⌐ **Joinery**
General joinery
Interior trim
Plywood

Ulmus americana
American elm

STRENGTHS
- Easy to use
- Finishes well
- Good substitute for other elms

WEAKNESSES
- Limited availability
- Ordinary color and patterning
- Grain can be interlocking and fibrous

THE SOFTER AND MORE SYMPATHETIC ELM

American elm, which is often referred to as white elm, is neither as popular nor as widely available as red elm (*U. rubra*). However, because it is softer and the grain tends to be more consistent, it is a little easier to work. It is usually employed as a utility lumber rather than as a quality hardwood for furniture and cabinetmaking, though it is often used as a substitute for red elm as long as strength is not a consideration.

KEY CHARACTERISTICS
Type Temperate hardwood
Other names White elm, soft elm, swamp elm, water elm, gray elm
Alternatives Spanish chestnut (*Castenea sativa*), other elms
Sources North America
Color Pale brown, with a slight reddish hue
Texture Coarse and soft, but even

Grain Straight, with a little interlocking, but the contrast between latewood and earlywood is less than for red elm (*U. rubra*).
Hardness Soft
Weight Medium (35 lb./cu. ft.) (560 kg/cu. m)
Strength Moderate, but very good for bending
Seasoning and stability Moderate
Wastage Medium
Range of board widths Good
Range of board thicknesses Good
Durability Prone to insect attack and rot when used outside

IN THE WORKSHOP
The main challenge with gray elm is that it is soft, so while it will not dull edges, it may tear and the woolliness may make it difficult to finish.

Milling Planes well, but do not try to remove too much in a pass, as it might tear.
Shaping Will not produce the sharpest of edges. This is a lumber designed for textural effects rather than precise profiles.
Assembly Good; screws, nails and glues well.
Finishing American elm is soft enough for power sanders to make dips in easily, so care needs to be taken.

VARIATIONS
Look out for mottled rays on quartersawn sides, and for burls.

SUSTAINABILITY
Not listed as endangered and not readily available as certified stock.

AVAILABILITY AND COST
Less readily available than red elm (*U. rubra*), but cheaper.

Key uses **Interior** Furniture   **Luxury & leisure** Sports equipment

 Marine Boat building Marine construction   **Utility** Coffins

Ulmus x hollandica
Dutch elm

STRENGTHS
- Marvelous figure and grain
- Luscious colors
- Soft, and ideal for chair seats

WEAKNESSES
- Increasingly rare
- Interlocking grain makes it difficult to work
- Not very stable

DISEASE-PRONE SPECIES ONCE FAVORED FOR SEATS AND TABLETOPS

Dutch elm disease has ripped through many forests and fields, and this beautiful tree is in continual decline. The lumber has a swirling grain and a wonderful range of colors. A wealth of knots add to the character, making this lightweight hardwood even trickier to work.

KEY CHARACTERISTICS

Type Temperate hardwood

Other names European elm, Holland elm

Related species English elm (*U. procera*), which is not as tough as Dutch elm and has a wilder grain

Alternatives Blackwood (*Acacia melanoxylon*), red maple (*Acer rubrum*), European plane (*Platanus hybrida*), American elm (*U. americana*)

Sources Grows across Europe

Color Pale honey, with some beige bands and light sapwood

Texture Relatively coarse-grained

Grain Growth rings of variable width combine with swirling grain

Hardness Soft for a hardwood

Weight Medium (35 lb./cu. ft.) (560 kg/cu. m)

Strength The European variety is stronger than the English elm and can be steam bent.

Seasoning and stability Moves moderately once used, and must be seasoned very carefully or the stack will collapse because of distortion.

Wastage Can be high, with defects, invasive bark and sapwood.

Range of board widths Variable

Range of board thicknesses Depends on the sawmill

Durability Needs preservative for external use; prone to insect attack indoors.

IN THE WORKSHOP

Dutch elm is prized more for its texture, figure and color than its structural qualities.

Milling Grain can tear. Beware of saws catching as the tension is removed from a board.

Shaping Tools must be kept sharp, but even so Dutch elm does not take a good edge, and other temperate hardwoods are better for cutting joints or routing profiles.

Assembly Elm must be given an opportunity to move when it is used as a panel, or as a tabletop or chair seat. Glues well and joints can be knocked very tight as it's fairly forgiving. Will not split from screws or nails.

Finishing Like many coarse-textured temperate hardwoods, elm is best given a wax finish that does not inhibit its natural softness.

VARIATIONS

Burl elm is a highly prized of burled woods. Quartersawn sides can exhibit dappling like lacewood.

SUSTAINABILITY

There is not much certified supply, but it is safe to use.

AVAILABILITY AND COST

It may be available from specialist importers, otherwise it must be bought as a veneer. The cost is lower than might be expected, but there is likely to be some wastage.

Key uses **Interior**
Chair seats
Tabletops
Cabinetmaking

 Marine
Boat building

Decorative
Turning
Burl elm is used as veneer for cabinetmaking and coachbuilding

Ulmus rubra
Red elm

STRENGTHS
- Subtle color and pattern
- Soft, textural effect
- Easy to work

WEAKNESSES
- Grain can be interlocking
- Supply limited by disease

TEXTURAL LUMBER LIMITED BY DISEASE
Red elm is darker and redder than American elm, and more like Dutch elm in color and texture. Unfortunately it too has suffered from Dutch elm disease, and supplies are increasingly limited. However, this splendid wood is still available and well worth hunting out. Elm is medium in weight, with an attractive wavy grain pattern and subtle medium brown color that darkens with age. The texture is far from fine, but it is ideal when you want to create a soft, textural effect.

KEY CHARACTERISTICS
Type Temperate hardwood
Other names Slippery elm, brown elm
Alternatives Other elms (*Ulmus* species), lacewood, which is found on the quartersawn sides of London plane (*Platanus accrifolia*).
Sources North America
Color Mid-brown with a reddish hue; some dark brown heartwood, but pale gray or white sapwood
Texture Coarse, but generally even

Grain Straight or gently wavy, with some interlocking grain, especially around knots
Hardness Soft to medium
Weight Medium (38 lb./cu. ft.) (610 kg/cu. m)
Strength Moderate
Seasoning and stability Slow to season, with some distortion, and moderate movement once dry.
Wastage Medium, with contrasting sapwood
Range of board widths Good when available
Range of board thicknesses Should be fine when available
Durability Poor

IN THE WORKSHOP
Red elm is a classic hardwood that woodworkers will want to use again and again once they have tried it. It has a subtle smell and works well enough.

Milling Though relatively soft, red elm planes well, with only a slight risk of tearing.
Shaping Not renowned for taking a sharp edge. Most users will decorate elm with softer, rounder profiles rather than attempting to cut sharp moldings. It cuts well for joints, however.
Assembly Easy to glue, nail and screw.
Finishing Finishes well, to a rich glow.

VARIATIONS
Burl elm is highly prized by turners and as veneer. Quartersawn sides can often feature mottled rays, not dissimilar to lacewood.

SUSTAINABILITY
Dutch elm disease is a greater risk to red elm than exploitation, and there is no great need to source certified supplies.

AVAILABILITY AND COST
Increasingly limited because of disease, but not especially expensive.

Key uses **Interior** Furniture and cabinetmaking Flooring **Utility** Coffins

 Decorative Turning

SECONDARY WOODS

Visit a woodworking friend and you are bound to find half a dozen woods that you know well, plus a few others that you do not notice so often. If the Principal Woods section represents the species we would all like to use, this section comprises lumbers that are for the most part less popular with wordworkers. Some are well-known but hard to find, others are difficult to work, and some have a similar and more popular relative in the Principal Woods section. However, all have a valuable place in the pantheon of woodworking species.

Acanthopanax ricinofolius
Castor aralia

STRENGTHS
- Straight grain
- Interesting pattern
- Economical

WEAKNESSES
- Weaker than ash
- Coarse grain

WEAK ASH-LIKE HARDWOOD USED FOR PLY

Castor aralia is very similar to ash in color, texture and grain pattern, but it lacks the whippy qualities that make white ash (*Fraxinus Americana*) or European ash (*F. excelsior*) popular for tool handles and sports equipment. Nor is it rated as highly as ash for steam bending to make furniture. With some resemblance to red elm (*Ulmus rubra*), castor aralia has a coarse texture and straight grain, and can be finished to a good luster. It shrinks considerably during seasoning and will continue to move and twist once dry. Being weaker than ash species and not particularly durable, it tends to be used mainly for interior trim and plywood.

KEY CHARACTERISTICS
Type Tropical hardwood
Other names *Kalopanax pictus*, *Kalopanax septemlobus*, Japanese ash, sen
Sources Japan, China, Korea, Sri Lanka
Color Creamy beige, with very little difference between sapwood and heartwood
Texture Coarse, with uneven earlywood and latewood grain
Grain Straight
Hardness Moderate
Weight Medium (36 lb./cu. ft.) (580 kg/cu. m)

AVAILABILITY AND SUSTAINABILITY
Generally used for plywood and interior trim, castor aralia is moderately priced for a hardwood. There is no evidence of its being endangered, nor of certified supplies being available.

Key uses

Joinery
Plywood
Interior trim and joinery
Store interiors

Luxury & leisure
Sports equipment

Aesculus hippocastanum
Horse chestnut

STRENGTHS
- Fine, even texture
- Unusual pale color

WEAKNESSES
- Interlocking grain
- Weak
- Limited availability

CLASSIC TREE OF THE ENGLISH COUNTRYSIDE

Look at the bark of a horse chestnut tree and you will notice the vicious spiral of the trunk. That characteristic is often repeated in the lumber, which generally has a wavy grain at best and is often interlocking or spiraling. You can find some interesting figure, but the wood is difficult to plane without tearing. This is a pity, as the color is interesting and the lumber is otherwise easy to work. Though horse chestnut is used a little in the production of furniture and cabinets, it is generally considered a utility lumber for utensils and packing crates. It is also cut for decorative veneers, especially where there is mottled figure. Horse chestnut seasons poorly and is not durable, but it stains, glues, nails and screws well. The trees dominate many parts of the English countryside.

KEY CHARACTERISTICS

Type Temperate hardwood
Related species Buckeye or yellow buckeye (*A. flava*) in the United States
Sources United Kingdom and Europe
Color White to cream, though it yellows with age
Texture Fine and even
Grain Usually spiraling, wavy and interlocking
Hardness Medium, and not very strong
Weight Medium (31 lb./cu. ft.) (500 kg/cu. m)

AVAILABILITY AND SUSTAINABILITY

Horse chestnut should be a good lumber widely used, but it is let down by its grain. Though there are plenty of trees, especially in the United Kingdom, it is not easily available on the commercial market, as is also true of buckeye in the United States. There are no obvious threats to horse chestnut, but no certified supplies.

Key uses

Utility
Utensils
Packing crates

Decorative
Decorative veneer
Carving
Turning

Brosimum paraense
Bloodwood

STRENGTHS
- Amazing color
- Fine, even texture

WEAKNESSES
- Limited dimensions
- Wide sapwood

COLORFUL COUSIN OF THE MULBERRIES

Bloodwood, often known as satine, belongs to the mulberry family (Moraceae). Few woods are so dramatic but also so uniform in color, and bloodwood is also wonderfully smooth and even in texture, perhaps because the tree grows so tall and straight. The color will diminish with age, and wide boards are not always available, but bloodwood is surprisingly easy to use and polishes up to a good luster.

KEY CHARACTERISTICS

Type Tropical hardwood
Other names *B. rubescens*, satine
Sources South America
Color Deep red, with yellow-white sapwood
Texture Fine to medium
Grain Straight, but occasionally interlocking
Hardness Hard
Weight Very heavy (60 lb./cu. ft.) (960 kg/cu. m)

AVAILABILITY AND SUSTAINABILITY

Not widely available, so you will need to hunt down specialty stores or online suppliers, and it is expensive. Bloodwood is often supplied as veneer. The sapwood is particularly wide, so boards may be very limited in width. Not listed as endangered.

Key uses

Interior
Furniture
Cabinetmaking

Decorative
Veneer
Inlay
Turning

▣— **Luxury & leisure**
Fishing rods

Caesalpinia echinata
Brazilwood

STRENGTHS
- Lovely color and texture
- Straight grain

WEAKNESSES
- Blunts tools
- Slow to dry

LUSTROUS HARDWOOD WITH GREAT COLOR

This is a beautiful wood, known by many names around the world. Do not expect the orange color to last; as with many species the initial hue darkens with age. Brazilwood can be smoothed to a fantastic finish with a high luster, but it can be awkward to work, mainly because it can dull the edges of tools. It is too hard to nail easily, but unlike some oilier species it glues well.

KEY CHARACTERISTICS

Type Tropical hardwood
Other names *Guilandina echinata*, para wood, Bahia wood, pau Brasil, fernambuco wood, Braziletto, pau ferro (which is also used as a name for jacaranda pardo [*Machaerium villosum*] and for Mexican brown ebony [*Libidibia sclerocarpa*])
Related species Partridgewood, Maracaibo ebony, granadillo (all *C. granadillo*)
Sources Brazil
Color Reddish brown, with dark lines and contrasting pale sapwood. The wood is initially a strong orange color, but darkens with time. There are often some knots.
Texture Fine to medium, and even
Grain Generally straight, but occasionally interlocking
Hardness Hard, with a high luster
Weight Very heavy (80 lb./cu. ft.) (1280 kg/cu. m)

AVAILABILITY AND SUSTAINABILITY

Though it is still available, Brazilwood has been listed by IUCN as endangered by exploitation, and supplies should be checked for sustainability. We have found no certified lumber.

Key uses **Luxury & leisure**
Violin bows
Gunstocks

 Interior
Flooring
Furniture

Decorative
Ornamental turning

Cedrela toona
Australian red cedar

STRENGTHS
- Mahogany substitute
- Good luster

WEAKNESSES
- Gum can clog cutters

MAHOGANY BY ANY OTHER NAME
Australian red cedar bears an uncanny resemblance to genuine mahogany (*Swietenia macrophylla*) but is more consistent and has a marvelous sheen or luster. The tree is tall and statuesque, while the lumber is light red, darkening with age. It is of medium weight and uniform in texture, and it works well apart from a small risk of cutters becoming clogged with gum. The wood is generally stable once seasoned.

KEY CHARACTERISTICS
Type Tropical hardwood
Similar species Mahogany (*Swietenia macrophylla*)
Sources India, Southeast Asia, Australia
Color Pale pink to light brown
Texture Medium to coarse, but uniform
Grain Straight, with some interlocking
Hardness Medium
Weight Medium to heavy (42 lb./cu. ft.) (670 kg/cu. m)

AVAILABILITY AND SUSTAINABILITY
No evidence of certified supplies, but this is not an endangered species, though environmentalists do warn woodworkers to avoid lumber from old-growth forests. Australian red cedar is likely to be moderately priced, but it is probably not widely available in North America.

Key uses **Interior** Furniture Cabinetmaking

Marine Boat building

Joinery Quality interior trim

Decorative Carving

Chloroxylon swietenia
Ceylon satinwood

STRENGTHS
- Subtle pattern and color
- High luster and smooth texture
- Stable

WEAKNESSES
- Tends to dull edges
- Not very strong

GLITTERING GOLD HARDWOOD THAT IS DIFFICULT TO WORK

View unfinished Ceylon satinwood under direct light and you will notice that it glitters, its tiny specks indicating the abrasive nature of the lumber. Though it finishes to a high luster and a subtle wavy grain, the species is difficult to work, largely because it dulls tools. It can have intriguing figure and shimmering defects. It is not particularly durable, but is attractive for paneling.

KEY CHARACTERISTICS
Type Tropical hardwood
Other names East Indian satinwood, flowered satinwood, buruta
Sources India, Sri Lanka
Color Pale yellow or straw, with darker tan or brown lines and bands
Texture Fine to medium, and largely, but not entirely, even
Grain Wavy
Hardness Hard
Weight Very heavy (61 lb./cu. ft.) (980 kg/cu. m)

AVAILABILITY AND SUSTAINABILITY

There are a number of different types of satinwood, so it is difficult to judge just how widely available Ceylon satinwood is, but it is not the most expensive type. However, there are reports of overexploitation and it has been listed as vulnerable, so it is worth considering a certified alternative.

Key uses

Interior
Furniture
Cabinetmaking

Joinery
Interior trim

Decorative
Turning
Inlay
Veneer

Dalbergia frutescens
Brazilian tulipwood

STRENGTHS
- Amazing color and pattern
- High luster

WEAKNESSES
- Limited dimensions available
- Expensive

STRIKING PINK AND RED ROSEWOOD RELATIVE

Though it is not as dark as many of the *Dalbergia* rosewoods, Brazilian tulipwood is nonetheless a distinctive and beautiful lumber. It should not be confused with tuliptree (*Liriodendron tulipifera*), which is sometimes known as tulipwood. One key drawback, however, is that it is available only in limited dimensions and may therefore suffer from instability. It finishes well but tends to splinter and crack, and even the veneer is likely to warp and split.

KEY CHARACTERISTICS
Type Tropical hardwood
Other names Pinkwood, pau rosa, bois de rose
Sources Brazil
Color Pale yellow or straw, with pink, red and brown streaks. Unfortunately the colors tend to fade with age.
Texture Fine to medium, and reasonably even
Grain Slightly wavy
Hardness Hard
Weight Heavy (60 lb./cu. ft.) (960 kg/cu. m)

AVAILABILITY AND SUSTAINABILITY
Surprisingly, Brazilian tulipwood has not been listed as endangered or vulnerable. However, it is likely to be expensive and is most easily bought as veneer.

Key uses **Interior**
Furniture
Cabinetmaking

Decorative
Turning
Veneer for paneling

Dracontomelon dao
Paldao

STRENGTHS
- Attractive color
- Distinctive grain pattern
- Can be straight-grained

WEAKNESSES
- Can have interlocking grain
- Medium to coarse texture

ASIAN HARDWOOD WITH A TOUCH OF WALNUT

Varying from brown through gray to black, paldao is distinguished by the inconsistent bands, stripes and lines that characterize the wide range of species known as walnut. Though not a true walnut, paldao has greater resemblance in color and patterning to English walnut (*Juglans regia*) than most of the other imposters from around the world, but the texture is coarser and the grain is more interlocking, which can make surfacing and finishing tricky.

KEY CHARACTERISTICS

Type Tropical hardwood
Other names *D. cumingiamum*, *D. edule*, New Guinea walnut, dao
Sources Southeast Asia
Color From pale brown and beige to gray, dark brown and black
Texture Medium to coarse
Grain Variable; straight or wavy and interlocking
Hardness Medium to hard, and stronger and tougher than the true walnuts (*Juglans* species)
Weight Medium to heavy (46 lb./cu. ft.) (740 kg/cu. m)

AVAILABILITY AND SUSTAINABILITY

Paldao is not too difficult to find and prices are likely to be moderate to expensive. It is not listed as vulnerable and is not overexploited.

Key uses **Interior**
Furniture
Flooring

 Joinery
Interior trim
Joinery
Store interiors

 Decorative
Veneer

Endiandra palmerstonii
Queensland walnut

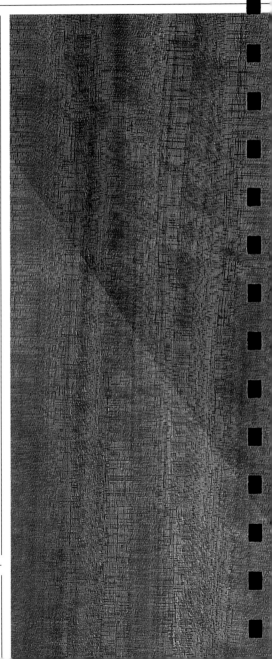

STRENGTHS
- Rich brown color
- Distinctive stripes

WEAKNESSES
- Poor grain
- Distorts during seasoning
- Abrasive

PRETEND WALNUT WITH INFERIOR STRIPES

Though it is not a true walnut, Queensland walnut has distinctive stripes that shimmer intriguingly, with the paler bands almost silvery beside the dark brown streaks. The lumber is often abrasive and can dull tool edges quickly. It has interlocking grain, making it difficult to work, and it does not season easily. In its favor, Queensland walnut finishes to a rich brown color. It is popular for furniture making and interior trim.

KEY CHARACTERISTICS

Type Tropical hardwood
Other names Australian walnut
Sources Australia
Color Medium brown, with darker stripes and some gray, pink or green streaks
Texture Medium
Grain Interlocking
Hardness Hard
Weight Medium to heavy (42 lb./cu. ft.) (670 kg/cu. m)

AVAILABILITY AND SUSTAINABILITY

Though it is rare outside Australia, Queensland walnut is not listed as one of the Australian species that are under threat.

Key uses **Interior**
Furniture
Cabinetmaking
Flooring

 Joinery
Interior trim

Entandrophragma utile
Utile

MAHOGANY IN ALL BUT NAME

Utile shares many of the characteristics of African mahogany, for which it is often used as a substitute. I have a soft spot for this lumber, as I used it to make my first toolbox, but I probably would not consider employing it again because it is difficult to work and not hugely attractive. It too has alternating bands of pale and medium red-brown, variable in width and length, which hint at interlocking grain, though it is probably more consistent than African mahogany.

KEY CHARACTERISTICS
Type Tropical hardwood
Sources Africa
Color Varying bands of pale and medium reddish brown that darken with age to a more consistent color
Texture Medium to coarse, but relatively even
Grain Straight, but can also be interlocking
Hardness Hard
Weight Medium to heavy (41 lb./cu. ft.) (660 kg/cu. m)

AVAILABILITY AND SUSTAINABILITY
Utile is not as widely available as African mahogany, but it is just as heavily exploited in Africa and is unlikely to be available from certified sources. It has been listed as vulnerable.

Key uses

🏠 **Interior**
Furniture
Cabinetmaking

⌐ **Joinery**
Store interiors
Interior trim

Eucalyptus gomphocephala
Tuart

STRENGTHS
- Good color and figure
- Strong and hard

WEAKNESSES
- Interlocking grain

HARD, PALE AND AUSTRALIAN

Though tuart used to be valued for making wagon wheels and propeller blades, it has declined significantly because so much of the tuart forest in Western Australia was cleared for grazing. It is a very heavy lumber without much patterning, but it has an intriguing color and some figure, and a grain that is largely straight but slightly interlocking. Tuart is often favored for making items that demand strength, because it is resistant to splitting.

KEY CHARACTERISTICS
Type Temperate hardwood
Sources Western Australia
Color Pale brown or tan, with some light and dark reddish streaks
Texture Medium and even
Grain Straight but slightly interlocking
Hardness Very hard
Weight Very heavy (64 lb./cu. ft.) (1020 kg/cu. m)

AVAILABILITY AND SUSTAINABILITY

Very limited supply in Australia, let alone elsewhere, though not particularly expensive. Certified supplies are unlikely to be found.

Key uses

 Interior Furniture

Technical Wheel making

 Decorative Turning

Khaya ivorensis
African mahogany

STRENGTHS
- Color of genuine mahogany
- Stable
- Economical

WEAKNESSES
- Difficult to work
- Variable grain and texture

MAHOGANY IN NAME AND COLOR BUT NOT IN SPIRIT

Identified by its pale and medium reddish brown bands, which are variable in width, African mahogany is one of the poorest of species to be honored with that famous name. It often has little shimmering figure. The texture is medium-coarse and somewhat uneven, reflecting the straight but interlocking grain. Though it is stable once seasoned, the lumber tends to tear badly when it is machined or worked by hand. Not particularly strong or durable, it is favored only as a substitute for finer mahoganies, and is often stained for reproduction furniture.

KEY CHARACTERISTICS

Type Tropical hardwood
Other names Khaya
Related species *K. anthotheca*, *K. grandifolia*, *K. nyasica*, *K. senegalensis*
Sources Africa
Color Reddish brown, varying from medium to pale
Texture Fairly coarse and uneven
Grain Straight, but also interlocking
Hardness Medium
Weight Medium (35 lb./cu. ft.) (560 kg/cu. m)

AVAILABILITY AND SUSTAINABILITY

African mahogany is not widely available and should be used with some caution and research because it has been listed as vulnerable by IUCN. The lumber is not usually expensive.

Key uses   **Interior**
Furniture
Cabinetmaking

Marine
Boat building

Joinery
Interior trim
Store interiors

Marmaroxylon racemosum
Marblewood

STRENGTHS
- Distinctive patterning
- High luster

WEAKNESSES
- Difficult to work
- Coarse texture

COARSE BUT LINED HARDWOOD

Marblewood, which is sometimes known as serpentwood, combines the patterning of zebrawood (*Microberlinia brazzavillensis*) with the color and coarse texture of English oak (*Quercus robur*). It even has some of oak's medullary rays, but not the shimmering flame. We have seen a warning to beware of the dust when working marblewood, but this is a good general rule, whatever the wood. It is not an easy lumber to work, with interlocking grain and a coarse texture that combine to challenge the woodworker, but it polishes to a high luster. It is perhaps best surfaced by sanding.

KEY CHARACTERISTICS

Type Tropical hardwood
Other names Serpentwood, angelim rojada, angelin rojada
Sources South America
Color Golden honey-brown interspersed with thinner dark brown, black or purple lines that meander across all the faces.
Texture Coarse and fairly uniform
Grain Straight, but also interlocking
Hardness Hard
Weight Heavy (c. 53 lb./cu. ft.) (850 kg/cu. m)

AVAILABILITY AND SUSTAINABILITY

Marblewood is rare and not easy to find, but neither is it terribly expensive. You may find certified supplies, as it is a lesser-known species that has not been exploited.

Key uses **Interior**
Furniture
Cabinetmaking

Decorative
Turning

Joinery
Paneling
Interior trim

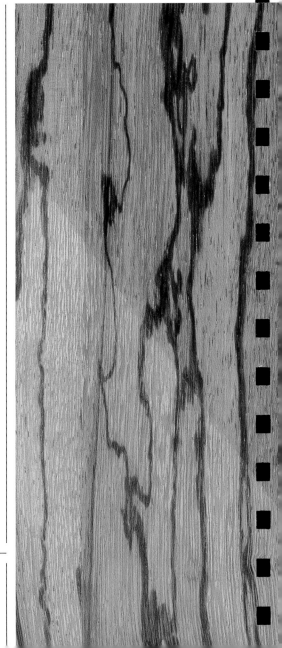

Millettia stuhlmannii
Panga panga

HARDWOOD THAT IS A LIGHTER SHADE OF WENGE

Very similar in looks, panga panga is related to the more famous black hardwood wenge (*M. laurentii*). The lumber has an intriguing mix of colors, from mid-gold to black streaks of gum. It has thin, dark brown lines like the medullary rays of oak, but these never flame in quite the same way. The effect is very dramatic on either quartersawn or plain-sawn sides. Panga panga is said to be stable in use, and its hardness and distinctive pattern make it ideal for parquet or strip flooring.

KEY CHARACTERISTICS
Type Tropical hardwood
Sources East Africa
Color Bands of dark and light brown with some gold and some black streaks
Texture Coarse and uneven
Grain The light and dark bands that give panga panga its distinctive look have a contrasting density that makes working difficult. There is also a risk of gum pockets that can clog blades. Otherwise the grain is generally straight, but sometimes interlocking.
Hardness Hard
Weight Heavy (58 lb./cu. ft.) (930 kg/cu. m)

AVAILABILITY AND SUSTAINABILITY
Not as widely available as wenge, and moderately expensive. Not listed as vulnerable.

Key uses

 Interior Furniture Flooring

Construction General construction

 Decorative Turning

 Joinery General joinery

Pinus ponderosa
Ponderosa pine

STRENGTHS
- Fine, evenly textured and stable sapwood

WEAKNESSES
- Resinous heartwood
- Tends to be knotty

SOFTWOOD VALUED FOR ITS SAPWOOD

Ponderosa pine has a split personality. The sapwood is silky to the touch, pale yellow in color and has subtle lines of earlywood and latewood that blend softly into one another with an even texture. The heartwood, however, is far more variable, being heavier and distinguished by dark resin lines. It can also be knotty and is not particularly strong or durable. The sapwood is stable and valued for specific purposes like patternmaking and carving, and veneer is cut from clean logs. With preservative it can be used outside. The main problem when working the lumber is that the heartwood is very resinous and likely to clog cutters and blades.

KEY CHARACTERISTICS

Type Temperate softwood
Other names Western yellow pine, knotty pine, bird's-eye pine, California white pine, Rocky Mountain yellow pine
Related species Jeffrey pine (*P. jeffreyi*), which is often sold as ponderosa pine
Sources Western United States and Canada
Color Pale yellow sapwood; darker heartwood with reddish brown resin lines
Texture Fine and even, particularly the sapwood, which is soft and easy to work
Grain Straight, but high risk of knots diverting the grain direction
Hardness Soft to medium for a softwood
Weight Medium (32 lb./cu. ft.) (510 kg/cu. m)

AVAILABILITY AND SUSTAINABILITY
Widely available and not listed as endangered.

Key uses **Decorative**
Patternmaking
Veneer
Carving

Construction
General construction

 Joinery
Interior trim

Populus *species*
Poplar

STRENGTHS
- Cheap
- Fast growing
- Light
- Doesn't split

WEAKNESSES
- Lacks luster
- Soft and woolly
- Can be full of defects
- Brittle

ROUGH LUMBER FOR BOXES AND CRATES

Poplar comes in many forms, which are occasionally referred to as aspen. However, it should not be confused with tuliptree (*Liriodendron tulipifera*), which is sometimes called yellow poplar. The various species of aspen and poplar are used primarily for utilitarian jobs such as rough framing, posts, boxes, crates, plywood and matches, but also for some interior trim work. The lumber is not suitable for furniture making. Nevertheless, it does not split when nailed and is light and relatively easy to work, so it's ideal for practical tasks.

KEY CHARACTERISTICS

Type Temperate hardwood
Other names European black poplar (U.K.), European aspen (U.S.), cottonwood
Species Eastern cottonwood (*P. deltoides*), trembling aspen (*P. tremuloides*), balsam poplar (*P. balsamifera*), *P. nigra*, *P. canadensis*, *P. robusta*, *P. tremula*
Alternatives American whitewood (*Liriodendron tulipifera*)
Sources Europe and North America
Color Irregular cream and brown bands with silvery interlocking patches at right angles to the grain pattern.
Texture Generally even, but neither fine nor coarse, and certainly fibrous.
Grain Generally straight, but can also be wavy and interlocking.
Hardness Soft
Weight Light (28 lb./cu. ft.) (450 kg/cu. m)

AVAILABILITY AND SUSTAINABILITY

It is safe to buy any aspen or poplar, whether or not it is certified. It is easy to acquire, and invariably cheap.

Key uses

  Joinery
Interior trim
Plywood

  Construction
General construction

  Exterior
Posts

  Utility
Packing cases
Crates
Boxes

Pterocarpus dalbergioides
Andaman padauk

STRENGTHS	WEAKNESSES
• Beautiful color and figure	• Interlocking grain
• Durable	• Difficult to season

NARRA IN NAME BUT NOT IN SPECIES

Andaman padauk is a pink or honey color and shares the look and feel of its relative amboyna (*P. indicus*), which is also often known as narra. Andaman padauk is not easy to season, and foresters girdle trees to reduce the risk of surface checking. It is durable and strong, but does not bend well. The interlocking grain can be awkward to work and the lumber can dull tools. In India it is used for construction and marine purposes.

KEY CHARACTERISTICS

Type Tropical hardwood
Other names Padauk, Andaman redwood, vermillion wood, red narra, yellow narra
Related species Narra or amboyna (*P. indicus*)
Sources Andaman Islands (in the Indian Ocean)
Color Variable, from pink with red streaks to brick red with purple streaks. The wood darkens to a red-brown; the paler honey-colored or pink boards are less common but highly prized.
Texture Medium to coarse, and relatively even
Grain Interlocking, with striped or mottled figure
Hardness Hard
Weight Medium to heavy (48 lb./cu. ft.) (770 kg/cu. m)

AVAILABILITY AND SUSTAINABILITY

P. dalbergioides is occasionally sold as narra by specialist sources, but the situation is confused by the fact that *P. indicus*, which is more usually referred to as narra or amboyna, is now in very short supply and is extinct in some Asian and Southeast Asian countries. There appears to be no current threat to Andaman padauk, but we have not been able to find certified *P. dalbergioides*. Any supplies will be limited and expensive.

Key uses

 Interior
Furniture
Cabinetmaking
Flooring
Work surfaces

 Decorative
Turning
Veneer

Marine
Boat building

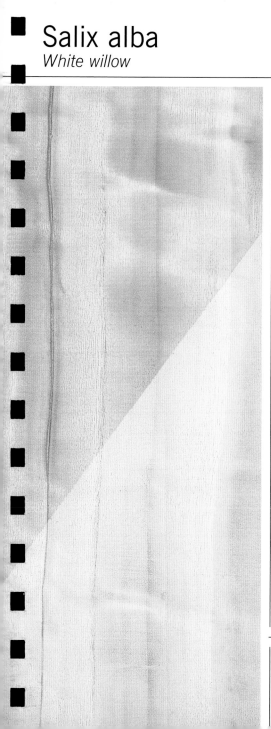

Salix alba
White willow

STRENGTHS
- Inexpensive
- Light and easy to work
- Versatile

WEAKNESSES
- Weak
- Not durable
- Bland color

A UTILITY LUMBER WITH A SPORTING HISTORY

Willow is not used commercially for much beyond cricket bats, though it is a useful utility lumber for mass-produced items and plywood, and it is also cut for decorative veneer. The patterning is subtle and boards are relatively easy to work, but as with other soft, fibrous species, tool edges must be very sharp. Willow lacks durability and strength and it cannot be bent without breaking.

KEY CHARACTERISTICS

Type Temperate hardwood
Other names Willow, common willow
Related species Black willow (*S. nigra*), crack willow (*S. fragilis*), cricket bat willow (*S. alba* var. *caerulea*)
Sources Europe, Middle East and North Africa; black willow (*S. nigra*) is grown in the United States
Color Pale cream to tan or light brown; often has shimmering silvery figure and some darker streaks or ring lines
Texture Uniformly fine
Grain Straight
Hardness Soft to medium
Weight Light (21–28 lb./cu. ft.) (340–450 kg/cu. m)

AVAILABILITY AND SUSTAINABILITY

Because willow is not a commercially important lumber, it is not widely available. It is, however, relatively cheap.

Key uses

 Utility
Utensils
Packaging and crates

Joinery
Plywood

Decorative
Decorative veneer

 Luxury & leisure
Cricket bats

Swietenia mahogani
Cuban mahogany

STRENGTHS
- Smooth, even texture
- Easy to work
- Beautiful color and pattern
- Stable and consistent

WEAKNESSES
- Almost extinct

A LESSON IN EXPLOITATION

Known as Cuban or Spanish mahogany, this wood is included here more as a lesson in overexploitation than for its commercial availability. Loved for its texture, patterning, stability and color, the species has been felled indiscriminately for the past five centuries and is now almost impossible to source. Nor has it been easy to regenerate or grow in plantations. If woodworkers need a reason to use a certified source for buying their favorite lumber, they should consider Cuban mahogany. Anyone who has recycled it (and that is the most likely source today) will recognize the inferiority of the other mahoganies that are available.

KEY CHARACTERISTICS

Type Tropical hardwood
Other names Spanish mahogany
Sources Recycled furniture only
Color Medium reddish brown that darkens with age
Texture Even and medium
Grain Straight
Hardness Medium
Weight Medium (34 lb./cu. ft.) (540 kg/cu. m)

AVAILABILITY AND SUSTAINABILITY

The only option now is to recycle broken furniture and recreate it as something new.

Key uses **Interior**
Fine furniture
Cabinetmaking

Decorative
Veneer

Tieghemella heckelii
Makoré

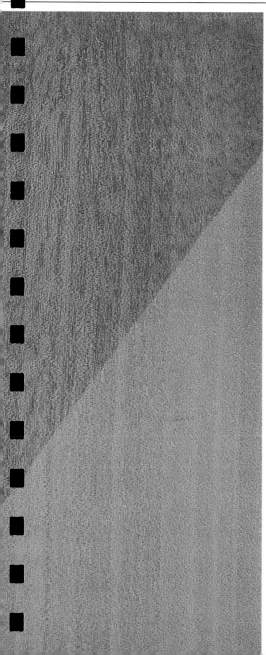

STRENGTHS
- Good color and figure
- Fine, even texture
- Stable

WEAKNESSES
- Can be brittle
- Endangered

SUPERB MAHOGANY SUBSTITUTE

Makoré is very similar to afzelia (*Afzelia cuanzensis*) and, like that wood, is used as a substitute for mahogany and now also cherry, which is becoming more expensive. Makoré is finer and has more figure to it than afzelia and is easier to finish to a high luster. However, it is more difficult to work than mahogany because it dulls tools and is more brittle. Keep it away from steel fittings, as it can be stained blue. Stable once dry, it is very durable, but is susceptible to attack by some insects.

KEY CHARACTERISTICS

Type Tropical hardwood
Other names *Mimusops heckelii, Dumoria heckelii,* cherry mahogany, African cherry, baku, babu, abaku
Related species *T. africana*
Sources West Africa
Color Deep reddish brown
Texture Fine and even
Grain Straight, but can also be more figured and mottled
Hardness Not particularly strong and moderately hard
Weight Medium (39 lb./cu. ft.) (620 kg/cu. m)

AVAILABILITY AND SUSTAINABILITY

Easy to source and moderately priced. Unfortunately it is classified as endangered, and we have not been able to find certified supplies, which should be considered if possible.

Key uses

 Interior
Furniture
Cabinetmaking
Flooring

Joinery
Quality interior trim

 Decorative
Veneer

Triplochiton scleroxylon
Obeche

STRENGTHS
- Even texture
- Stable
- Lightweight

WEAKNESSES
- Bland
- Weak

HARDWOOD USUALLY HIDDEN FROM VIEW

Obeche is generally used where it will not be seen or where strength and protection are not important. It is favored for frames within items of furniture that require lightweight components, such as ready-to-assemble chests and cabinets. With a uniform texture and interlocking but essentially straight grain, it is ideal for making thin items, such as moldings, that do not have to be finished to a high polish or luster. Obeche is surprisingly easy to work. It is stable, quick and easy to season. The only time the lumber is valued for its appearance, however, is when it is to be stained.

KEY CHARACTERISTICS

Type Tropical hardwood
Other names Ayous, samba, African whitewood, soft satinwood, wawa, bush maple, African maple, African primavera
Sources West Africa
Color Pale honey or tan, sometimes almost yellow
Texture Medium and uniform
Grain Looks straight, with stripes when quartersawn, but usually interlocking
Hardness Medium
Weight Light (24 lb./cu. ft.) (380 kg/cu. m)

AVAILABILITY AND SUSTAINABILITY

Readily available, especially for mass production, and inexpensive. It does not appear to be threatened.

Key uses **Interior**
Mass-produced
furniture

Joinery
Plywood

Utility
Packaging

Turreanthus africanus
Avodire

GLOWING AFRICAN HARDWOOD WITH GOLDEN LUSTER

Often referred to as African satinwood, avodire is a rich golden honey color with a gently curving grain pattern. The grain hides interlocking sections that will challenge woodworkers. The lumber finishes to a superb luster and has a medium texture that is generally uniform. Quarter-sawn surfaces can be particularly attractive, with some mottled figure. Avodire is not as heavy or as hard and strong as you might expect, but it is a useful species for high-quality joinery and store interiors, with some use in furniture making. The veneer is used for marquetry but it does not stain consistently.

KEY CHARACTERISTICS
Type Tropical hardwood
Other names African satinwood
Sources West Africa, particularly Ghana, Cameroon, Nigeria, Congo and Ivory Coast
Color Golden honey to yellow
Texture Medium and fairly even
Grain Generally wavy or straight, but with some interlocking sections
Hardness Moderate
Weight Medium (34 lb./cu.ft.) (540 kg/cu. m)

AVAILABILITY AND SUSTAINABILITY
Avodire is not widely available but is medium priced. However, IUCN has reported it to be vulnerable to extinction, and we have not found certified supplies.

Key uses   **Joinery**
Store and office interiors
Plywood

 Decorative
Veneer for marquetry

SPECIAL EFFECTS

Though many woodworkers yearn for straight-grained lumber that is easy to plane and neat to work, there is often an irresistible challenge in working with trickier boards and with wood that displays the most decorative grain, patterning, color and texture. The majority of these effects are created by using veneers, with which we have chosen to illustrate this section, but woodturners and carvers also like to employ burls, figured and diseased sections. And given the opportunity, most furniture makers will opt for the beauty and stability of quartersawn boards.

Diseased Wood

The logging and lumber industries generally consider it good practice to remove felled trees from the forest quickly and convert them into planks to season. Many woodworkers value clean, straight, defect-free lumber for its strength, consistency and ease of use. However, not all lumber is so easy to manage, and not all woodworkers are so easy to please. Things go wrong in woodlands and those of us who regard woodworking as a creative pursuit can benefit greatly from the remarkable transformations that can happen.

Throughout this book you will find mentions of the high value that is placed on boards that have been altered by natural staining, disease or fungus. The handful of examples shown here illustrate some of the causes and consequences of wood behaving badly. Many are available only as veneers, but others, like the spalted woods, are popular with woodturners and can be acquired cheaply because they are easy to find and considered rotten by other woodworkers.

BOG OAK (*Quercus robur*)
Sunken oaks, thousands of years old, are revealed in bogs from time to time as pickled trees, incredibly hard and black or very dark brown.

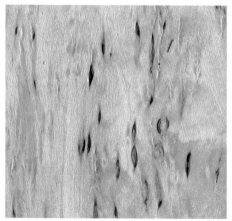

KARELIAN BIRCH (*Betula* species)
The flecks in Karelian birch are very similar to those in Masur birch, and are believed to be caused by insect attack or some other shock or injury.

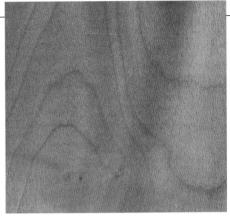

OLIVE ASH (*Fraxinus* species)
The center of ash logs often turns a dark brown. Darkest at the pith, it thins to streaks farther out. The effect can be dramatic and is much sought after, but frustrating.

WEATHERED SYCAMORE
(*Acer pseudoplatanus*)
Freshly cut sycamore is pure white, a color that is best maintained by fast seasoning. If it is dried more slowly a pinkish brown color can be achieved.

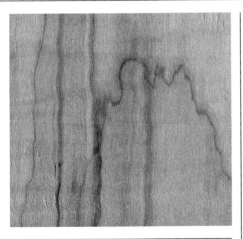

SPALTED MAPLE (*Acer saccharum or A. rubrum)*
Some species are prone to a disease that causes spalting: wavy colored lines that curl through the wood and are present in the boards cut from them.

BROWN ENGLISH OAK (*Quercus robur and Q. petraea)*
This is similar to bog oak, but much lighter in color and a richer brown. The effect is caused by fungus, a bit like olive ash, and will often start from the pith.

Figured Wood

Figure is a confusing word for woodworkers in that it has both general and specific meanings. In its broadest sense, figure refers to a particularly interesting grain pattern in a board, beyond what you would normally expect. When used specifically, the word describes shimmering bands or streaks that usually run at right angles to the grain direction. They can be confused with medullary rays, but are in fact more subtle.

Though figure is the most common term, there are other words that describe particular effects. *Fiddleback* is similar, but more pronounced and regular, a bit like the scales on a mackerel, while *curly* is more open and less obvious. *Mottled* figuring is much more blotchy and random, while *lacewood* displays the remarkable flecking of medullary rays revealed by quartersawing. All these effects vary in intensity from one board to the next, and you will often find them labeled as "light" or "heavy" depending on the strength of figuring.

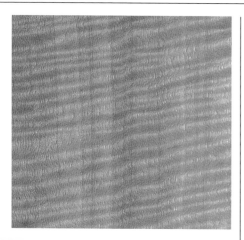

HEAVY-FIGURED ANINGERIA *(Aningeria superba)*
The contrast between this and light-figured aningeria is obvious, though you can see the clear similarities in the grain pattern and color.

LIGHT-FIGURED ANINGERIA *(Aningeria superba)*
This subtle figuring is visible only when you play a light on the surface, but it adds an extra dimension to a bland wood. This lumber is often known as anigre or anegré.

FIDDLEBACK SAPELE *(Entandrophragma cylindricum)*
Viewing fiddleback sapele from different angles produces remarkable effects, with the surface transforming itself as you move around. Notice the shorter lines of figuring.

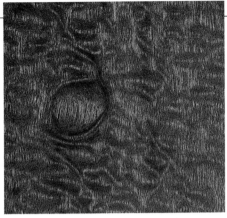

BLISTERED SAPELE *(Entandrophragma cylindricum)*
Whereas burl lumber derives from growths on trees, figuring occurs within the trunks and branches, but sometimes the effect is very similar.

FIDDLEBACK MAKORÉ *(Tieghemella heckelii)*
Fiddleback or figured effects are usually most conspicuous on quartersawn faces, in which the bands are narrower and more concentrated.

POMMELE MAKORÉ *(Tieghemella heckelii)*
One of the terms suppliers use to describe a mottled effect is pommele, which means a velvety look. Pommele with greater depth is sometimes referred to as drape.

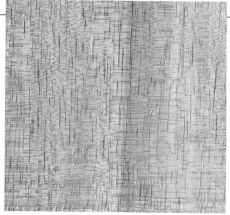

FIGURED ENGLISH OAK *(Quercus robur* and *Q. petraea)*

Oak is not commonly associated with figuring, but the growth rings can sometimes have jagged edges, which are seen most easily on plain-sawn boards.

FIGURED KOA *(Acacia koa)*

This quartersawn koa displays thin lines of shimmering figure at right angles to the grain. It is ideal for panels or tops because the effect is subtle but interesting.

FIGURED WHITE EUCALYPTUS (*Eucalyptus* species)

White eucalyptus veneer, which cannot be linked to any one eucalyptus species, is available in figured form with spaces of ray figure on quartersawn faces.

FIGURED RED EUCALYPTUS (*Eucalyptus* species)

Similar to Red River gum (*Eucalyptus camaldulensis*), this figured red eucalyptus has the same figuring as white eucalyptus, with some of it unusually following the grain.

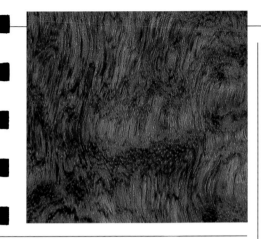

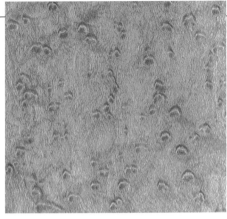

POMMELE BUBINGA *(Guibourtia demeusii)*
This veneer is rotary cut, peeled from the outside of the log, and displays bubinga's tendency to wavy, interlocking grain, which in this case is truly wild.

HEAVY BIRD'S-EYE MAPLE *(Acer saccharum or A. rubrum)*
This is regarded as a heavy example of bird's-eye figuring, with tiny pithy explosions that are tightly packed. It is thought to be caused by insect attack.

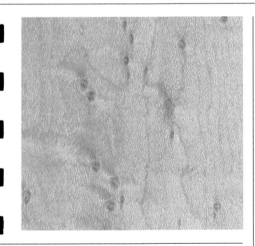

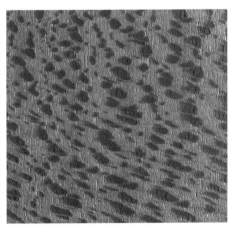

LIGHT BIRD'S-EYE MAPLE *(Acer saccharum or A. rubrum)*
The density of bird's-eye figuring varies from board to board, and you can find light bird's-eye on many boards. The grain often shines around areas of figuring.

LACEWOOD *(Platanus acerifolia)*
Most commonly found in London plane, lacewood describes the tight mottling found on the quartersawn sides of many species. It is particularly strong and regular in plane.

FIGURED AMERICAN MAHOGANY *(Swietenia macrophylla)*

Figuring can be symptomatic of interlocking grain and can predict difficulties with planing. In mahogany the figure tends to be inconsistent and concentrated.

FIGURED BIRCH *(Betula alleghaniensis)*

Most species have some form of figuring, but in some, like birch, it is indistinct. However, it does give an otherwise bland lumber an unexpected depth.

FIGURED CHERRY *(Prunus serotina)*

Black cherry has become one of the most popular species over the last 20 years, though it is not a wood with which figuring is associated.

FIGURED WHITE OAK *(Quercus alba)*

This veneer has been rift-sawn, at a slight angle to the growth rings, giving the effect of quartersawn boards without the flaming rays.

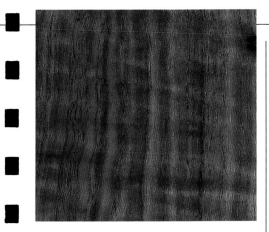

FIGURED BLACK WALNUT *(Juglans nigra)*
This veneer is more varied in color than some black walnut, and the figuring enhances the effect, giving it the look of European walnut (*J. regia*).

FIGURED PLANETREE MAPLE *(Acer pseudoplatanus)*
One of the best-known examples of figuring, and certainly one of the most dramatic, this is typified by tightly packed figure bands that narrow gently to thin points.

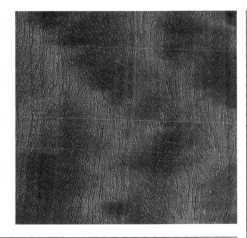

MOTTLED MAKORÉ *(Tieghemella heckelii)*
Rivers of shimmering grain wander across the surface of this veneer, changing constantly as you alter your angle of view. Figuring can indicate problems with interlocking grain, but generally does not have much effect.

FIGURED EUROPEAN BEECH *(Fagus sylvatica)*
As with birch, figuring in beech tends to be indistinct and quite rare, but it does give the uninteresting pattern of this famous English wood more subtlety.

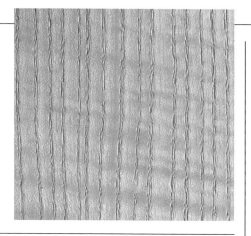

FIGURED EUROPEAN ASH (Fraxinus excelsior)
Figured ash is quite similar to figured sycamore (Acer pseudoplatanus) but it does not taper in the same way. It lacks sycamore's purity and simplicity.

MOTTLED SAPELE (Entandrophragma cylindricum)
Sapele has a marvelous selection of figuring options, with the mottled effect displaying a hologram of contrasting patterning that is relatively common in the species.

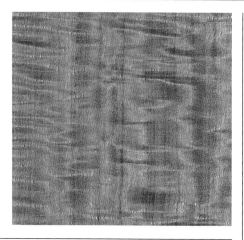

FIGURED WHITE PEROBA (Paratecoma peroba)
In this amazing example of figuring the spiky figure combines with medullary rays that run at right angles to the grain. The wood is quartersawn.

CROTCH AFRICAN MAHOGANY (Khaya ivorensis)
Crotch wood is cut from the junction between a branch and the trunk of a tree. The grain is random; you might be working with both long-grain and end-grain.

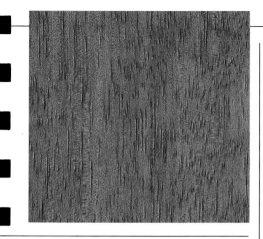

FIGURED PAU AMARELLO *(Euxylophora paraensis)*

On a lumber with virtually no visible grain pattern, the figure is important. In this case it is extremely subtle and hardly noticeable.

CURLY MAPLE *(Acer saccharum* or *A. rubrum)*

Maple is a genus that is commonly associated with figuring, and curly maple is very popular for furniture making. The effect is soft and flowing.

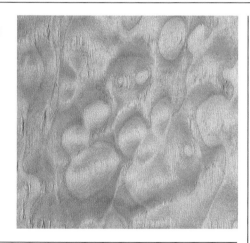

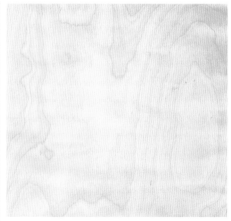

QUILTED MAPLE *(Acer saccharum* or *A. rubrum)*

Extraordinary shapes are found in quilted maple, almost like giant bird's eyes, giving the effect of small puddles of mercury running across the surface of the board.

ICE BIRCH *(Betula* species)

One of the many types of figuring to affect birch is known as ice figure. The term describes the very open patterning that is hardly noticeable on this plain-sawn piece.

Burls

Known as burrs in the United Kingdom, burls come from growths that form on trees like cancers and are caused by the loss of a branch or a wound to the bark. The grain is typically wild and very dense, so is particularly popular for turning, but you can also find cavities within a burl. The tightness of the burl can vary greatly. Burls are valuable and are often sliced for veneer; there are even reports of poachers with chainsaws stealing burls from living trees.

Burl veneers can be difficult to use because they are so twisted and buckled. They often need to be dampened to be flattened, and will commonly split when glued in place. You will need to cope with splits and cavities, though many woodworkers use them as a special effect to reveal a contrasting substrate (the ground or core to which veneer is glued). Burl veneers are superb for making boxes. Pips look like tiny knots, similar to the effect found in bird's-eye maple.

CARPATHIAN ELM BURL (*Ulmus* species)
Burls are so varied in color and pattern that the species is not always clear, as is the case with Carpathian elm burl. Notice the bird's-eye pips and wild, wavy grain.

MAHOGANY ROOT BURL (*Swietenia macrophylla*)
Burls can be found attached to the roots of mahogany trees, where the grain is likely to be wild anyway. In this case the pattern is surprisingly regular for a burl.

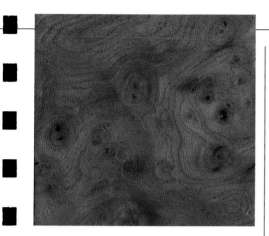

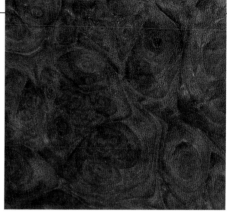

DUTCH ELM BURL *(Ulmus procera* or *U. hollandica)*

Notice the rich red color and the contours of pips and rivers that make many burls, and this one in particular, look like maps.

ENGLISH WALNUT BURL *(Juglans regia)*

As a veneer, English burl is extremely difficult to control, buckling wildly. In this example the effect is more regular than in some burls, with a series of close-spaced oysters.

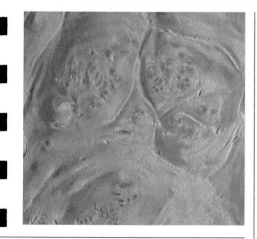

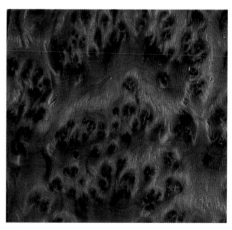

MAPLE CLUSTER *(Acer saccharum* or *A. rubrum)*

A combination of bird's-eye maple and quilted maple, this veneer shows very little grain but has a bright ray-like figure around the clusters of bird's-eye pips.

THUYA BURL *(Tetraclinis articulata)*

Now available only as a veneer, thuya burl comes from the root system of the thuya tree, which grows in North Africa. It is one of a few woods that are known only for their veneer.

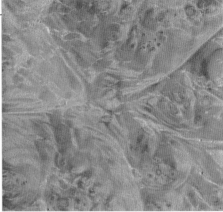

REDWOOD BURL *(Sequoia sempervirens)*
This is an extraordinary burl, with widely contrasting effects. At the heart of the burl the patterning is compact, but it then spreads into elongated shapes toward the edge, where the burl meets the tree.

MAPLE BURL *(Acer saccharum or A. rubrum)*
Notice the slight difference between maple burl and maple cluster. The former is one of the most dramatic of burls, and a contrast to the grainier burls of, say, elm.

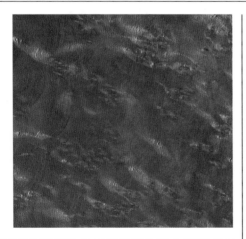

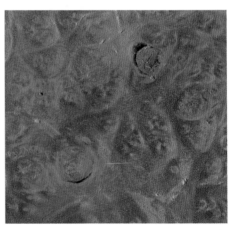

MADRONE BURL *(Arbutus menziesii)*
Madrone, a North American hardwood, produces a subtle, even burl that is ideal for marquetry because of its small but consistent patterning.

MYRTLE BURL *(Umbellularia californica)*
This delicious mid-brown burl is similar in color and patterning to amboyna or narra *(Pterocarpus indicus)*, but more widely available and less expensive.

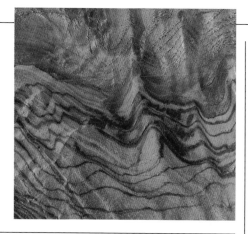

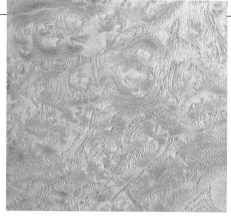

OLIVE ASH BURL *(Fraxinus excelsior)*
This combination of a burl with a disease creates a
stunning effect, with the brown lines of olive ash blending
with the quilting and wild grain of the burl. It is very
inconsistent in color and pattern.

WHITE ASH BURL *(Fraxinus americana)*
This example is highly concentrated, with the
characteristic ash grain still visible and running like
streams between the hillocks of concentrated grain. Note
the random pips.

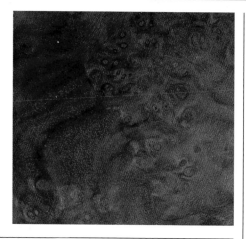

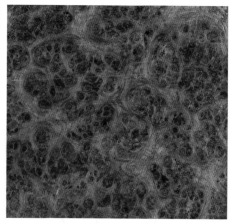

BLACK WALNUT BURL *(Juglans nigra)*
Far less dramatic than European walnut burls (*J. regia*),
this American example has a more even color – typical of
the species – smaller, pippy patterning and a wavy grain.

AMBOYNA BURL *(Pterocarpus indicus)*
One of the most splendid burls, amboyna is similar to
thuya burl (*Tetraclinis articulata*), but more golden in
color and tighter in pattern, resembling a microscopic
view of bacteria hurtling around a slide.

Quartersawn Surfaces

As explained earlier in this book, the most stable boards are quartersawn, with the growth rings running at right angles to the face. This reduces the risk of cupping, limits the greatest movement to the thickness and helps reduce movement across the width of a board. Quartersawn boards are particularly useful for items that require excellent stability, such as drawer components, and when wide boards cannot be held flat by a frame.

Typically, quartersawn faces are identified not only by the vertical growth rings in the end-grain but also by stripes of grain on the face. This can lead to quartersawn surfaces being rather uninteresting in some cases, though medullary rays, which run laterally through the tree, can be revealed in amazing flame patterns that shine and shimmer.

MACASSAR EBONY (*Diospyros celebica*)
Quarter- and plain-sawn surfaces of this classic species are not markedly different, though the grain pattern tends to be straighter and more regular on quartersawn lumber.

BLACK WALNUT (*Juglans nigra*)
Black walnut's beautiful straight grain and subtle variety of color are better displayed on quartersawn than plain-sawn surfaces. Quartersawn boards are not very common, however.

EUROPEAN BEECH *(Fagus sylvatica)*
The ray flecks in beech are never as conspicuous as the rays' flame in oak, and the grain is often almost invisible, but this unstable hardwood benefits from being quartersawn.

ANINGERIA *(Aningeria superba)*
As can be seen in this lovely example, aningeria has graduated growth rings of varying width, with subtle changes in color that darken and then are suddenly separated by thin, bright lines.

WHITE LIMBA *(Terminalia superba)*
Figured effects are often found on the quartersawn faces of limba. The species varies greatly in color, with dark limba showing dark brown lines and bands.

RED ELM *(Ulmus rubra)*
Plain-sawn boards of elm are typified by soft wavy lines and patterns, but quartersawing reveals straight grain and varying degrees of lacewood mottling.

WHITE OAK *(Q. alba)*

Considered less dramatic than European oak (*Quercus robur*), white oak still reveals the same flamed medullary rays on the quartersawn sides. In this example the rays are regular.

TEAK *(Tectona grandis)*

Though it is a beautiful and very durable hardwood, teak is not renowned for its patterning, but the quartersawn surfaces often show thin black lines at irregular intervals.

WESTERN HEMLOCK *(Tsuga heterophylla)*

The gently waving grain on quartersawn hemlock is densely packed, with thin red latewood lines that contrast with the paler earlywood. Notice the occasional darker bands.

BLACK CHERRY *(Prunus serotina)*

One of the beauties of black cherry is the lacewood effect that is revealed on quartersawn surfaces, but it happens only across limited areas when cut at a particular angle.

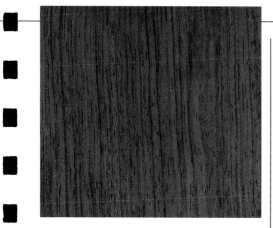

BUBINGA *(Guibourtia demeusei)*
Note the contrast between pommele bubinga and this quartersawn example, which is consistent and straight for a species that is often considered wild and varied.

CEYLON SATINWOOD *(Chloroxylon swietenia)*
This ribbon effect, with bands of contrasting color, is often found on quartersawn faces of satinwood. This example is unusual, with subtle golden colors and lines.

SAPELE *(Entandrophragma cylindricum)*
Sapele is known for its many figured effects, and even on this quartersawn example you can see the vertical silvery bands that are often revealed across the grain.

RED OAK *(Quercus rubra)*
This example shows how oak's medullary rays can vary greatly in pattern and effect, depending largely upon the angle of cut. A rift cut reduces the amount of ray flame.

Glossary

BLAND Uninteresting or undistinguished grain pattern, often associated with species that have fine, even texture and no obvious growth rings.

BOOK MATCHING Veneers from the same piece of wood are sometimes joined along their edges as mirror images of one another, either in pairs or in fours. Book matching is often used on box lids and tabletops, and for panels.

BURL Known as a burr in the United Kingdom, a burl is a growth on a tree trunk, branch or root that has tight, swirling grain, resembling a mass of knots. The wood in burls is often far denser than in the rest of the tree. Burls are used for veneer or by turners.

CASE-HARDENED In timber seasoning this term describes boards that have dried too quickly. The outside dries faster than the inside, causing all sorts of tensions that result in shakes, checks and honeycombing.

CHECKS Tiny splits on the surface of or within a board. Those that occur within the board during seasoning are often referred to as honeycombing, and you will sometimes hear checks referred to as checking.

CORE The wood to which veneer is applied is sometimes referred to as the core. Normally it is veneered on both sides, as application of a veneer on one side only will cause the core to distort.

CROWN-CUT Often described as plain-sawn or flat-sawn – or, in the United Kingdom, as through-and-through – crown-cut boards show the flame of growth rings, which often run horizontally across the board, and are signified by flat or slightly curving rings in the end-grain.

CSA Canadian Standards Association

DEGRADE If lumber is allowed to season too quickly or in the wrong conditions, it can suffer from splits, checks, staining, decay and a honeycombing effect that results in many tiny splits that rip the fibers apart. Collectively this sort of damage is referred to as degrade.

EARLYWOOD During the spring, trees add a more permeable tissue to carry nutrients and moisture from the ground to the leaves. This earlywood is often paler and softer than the darker bands of latewood, which is denser and designed to give the tree strength.

END-GRAIN The end of a board, which shows the curve of the growth rings. The end-grain is far harder to work than the long-grain.

FIDDLEBACK One of the many types of figure, fiddeback cuts often display a rippled effect, not unlike the patterning of a mackerel's scales.

FIGURE A general term to describe the patterning of wood, but more specifically the slightly more unusual effects that you can find in some boards. A woodworker might describe a board with particularly interesting patterning as having good figure, but to say it is figured refers more commonly to distinctive markings that often run at right angles to the grain direction.

HAREWOOD Sycamore wood that is chemically stained to a gray color.

IUCN The International Union for the Conservation of Nature, or World Conservation Union, has nearly 900 members comprising nations, government agencies and non-governmental organizations. It aims to promote conservation of the integrity and diversity of nature and the sustainable use of resources. The IUCN worked closely with the World Conservation Monitoring Centre (WCMC) in Cambridge, U.K., to produce *The World List of Threatened Trees*, published in 1998.

LACEWOOD When some woods are quartersawn a mottled effect is revealed in the section through the medullary rays. In some woods, like maple and elm, the effect is very subtle, but in others it is regular and distinctive. The classic examples are European or London plane (*Platanus acerifolia*) and roupala (*Roupala brasiliensis*). These species are often referred to as lacewood, so check which it is you are buying.

LATEWOOD The darker growth rings in many species that are added each year during the summer to give the tree strength.

LEI Lembaga Ekolabel Indonesia

MEDULLARY RAYS Extended cells that form within the tree at right angles to the grain direction in order to send nutrients horizontally across the tree. Medullary rays are often revealed in quartersawn surfaces as wild flames (as in oak) or as lacewood.

MOTTLING
A term used to describe various figuring effects, from subtle lacewood to a more velvety figuring.

MTCC Malaysian Timber Certification Council

OYSTERS A few woods are cut into oysters, which are a cross-section of end-grain either at right angles to the grain or at an oblique angle. The term refers particularly to laburnum (*Laburnum anagyroides*), which has contrasting sapwood and heartwood, though sometimes only the heartwood is used for oysters. They are laid out side by side in multiples on tabletops and panels.

PEFC Programme for the Endorsement of Forest Certification Schemes, which was formerly known as the Pan European Forest Certification Scheme.

RIBBON FIGURE On quartersawn surfaces the stripes of latewood and earlywood are sometimes referred to as ribbon figure, especially when there is a subtle range of color and the division between the stripes is also gentle.

RIPPLED CUTS Ripple figure is similar to fiddleback, with which it is easily confused, but the lines of ripple figure tend to be longer and straighter.

SAPWOOD Each year a tree grows a new layer of cells that carry sap, moisture, minerals and nutrients up and down the tree. Gradually the sapwood, which is often pale in color, is converted into heartwood, which is usually darker and harder. Sapwood is usually discarded by woodworkers, because it is often soft and also prone to insect attack. The proportion of sapwood to heartwood is the same throughout a tree's life, but varies from species to species.

SFI Sustainable Forestry Initiative

SHAKES Shakes are very similar to checks, but usually wider and longer. They generally work from the heart of the tree outward, at right angles rather than parallel to the growth rings.

SHORT-GRAIN Wood is strong and pliable because the fibers are long. Woods with shorter grain tend to be more brittle and easier to break. The term also refers to situations where the grain is weak and easily snapped, say in furniture or carving.

SLICING Some veneers, known as rotary-cut, are produced by peeling a thin film of wood from a rotating log, while others are made by slicing through the grain to reveal different grain patterns and effects. Slicing generally refers to the cutting of any veneer, but more specifically to non-rotary-cut types.

WANEY EDGES The irregular natural edges that are sometimes left on boards that are cut along the length of the log (plain- or flat-sawn, or crown-cut). One or two edges can be left waney, though this practice is much more common in Europe than in North America.

WAVY GRAIN When the fibers in a tree curve gently as they rise, as in European walnut (*Juglans regia*), the grain is known as wavy. A board cut from such a tree will have inconsistent grain direction, and the woodworker will face the challenge of working with and then against the grain.

WCMC World Conservation Monitoring Centre, Cambridge, U.K. (see IUCN on facing page).

WILD GRAIN Similar to wavy grain, but the inconsistency of the grain is more intense.

Index

Credits

Author's acknowledgements

With so many species featured in this book it was a challenge sourcing and preparing samples. For that Phil Davy must take great credit, for trawling his way through lumberyards to find boards of this and that, and then working with an enormous variety of wood types to produce finished boards.

Veneers were used to illustrate the special effects section and some of the lesser known species. These were supplied by Art Veneers in the U.K. (www.artveneers.co.uk) and Wood River Veneer, based in Idaho, U.S. (www.woodriverveneer.com). Frank Boddy at John Boddy's Fine Wood Store (www.john-boddy-timber.ltd.uk) kindly supplied us with samples we couldn't find elsewhere. Many thanks to all companies for their help.

Various organizations, people and businesses provided us with information or samples and are listed below. Many thanks for their contributions.

Adirondacks Hardwoods (www.adirondackwood.com)
Almquist Lumber (www.almquistlumber.com)
American Hardwood Export Council (www.ahec.org)
Andrews Timber and Plywood (tel. +44 (0)1277 657167)
Art Veneers (www.artveneers.co.uk)
Atkins & Cripps (www.atkinsandcripps.co.uk)
Capital Crispin Veneer (capveneer@aol.com)
Cascadia Forest Goods (www.cascadiaforestgoods.com)
Compton Lumber & Hardware (www.comptonlbr.com)
Craft Supplies (www.craft-supplies.co.uk)
Ecotimber (www.ecotimber.co.uk)
Eisenbrand Exotic Hardwoods (www.eisenbran.com)
Fauna and Flora (www.fauna-flora.org)
Friendly Forest Products (www.exotichardwood.com)
Gilmer Wood Co. (gilmerwood@aol.com)
Global Wood Source (www.globalwoodsource.com)
Good Timber (www.goodtimber.com)
Hardwood Store of North Carolina (www.hardwoodstore.com)
Inchope Madeiras (www.woodmarket.com)

John Boddy's Fine Wood Store (www.john-boddy-timber.ltd.uk)
Mark Corke (www.markcorkephotography.com)
North American Wood Products (www.nawpi.com)
Northland Forest Products (www.northlandforest.com)
O'Shea Lumber (www.oshealumber.com)
Precious Woods (www.preciouswoods.ch)
Rockler Woodworking Store (www.rockler.com)
Softwood Export Council (www.americansoftwoods.com)
TBM Hardwoods (www.tbmhardwoods.com)
Timber Development Association of South Australia (www.nafi.com.au/timbertalk)
Timberline (tel. +44 (0)1732 355626)
Trada (www.trada.co.uk)
U-Beaut Enterprises (www.ubeaut.biz)
U.S. Forest Products Laboratory (www.fpl.fs.fed.us)
Whitmore's Timber Co. (www.whitmores.co.uk)
Woodbin (www.woodbin.com)
Wood Explorer (www.woodexplorer.com)
Woodfinder (www.woodfinder.com)
Wood River Veneer (www.woodriverveneer.com)
The Wood & Shop Inc. (www.woodnshop.com)
Wood World (www.woodfibre.com)
Yandles (www.yandle.co.uk)

Quarto would like to thank and acknowledge the following for supplying photographs reproduced in this book:

(Key: t top, b bottom)
7	John Kelly/GETTY IMAGES
9	Rob Melnychuk/GETTY IMAGES
12t	Edward Parker
12b	N C Turner/FSC/WWF-UK
14	Fired Earth www.firedearth.com
19	Ecotimber
26t	Ecotimber

All other illustrations and photographs are the copyright of Quarto Publishing plc. While every effort has been made to credit contributors, Quarto would like to apologize should there have been any omissions or errors – and would be pleased to make the appropriate correction for future editions of the book.